DISTILLING ROB

MANLY LIES AND WHISKY TRUTHS

ROBERT L. GARD

To Harold,
I hope you enjoy this tale
of whisky and life!

WGR PUBLISHING
LOS ANGELES, CA

Copyright © 2013 by Robert L. Gard.

All rights reserved. No part of this publication may be reproduced, distributed or transmitted in any form or by any means, including photocopying, recording, or other electronic or mechanical methods, without the prior written permission of the publisher, except in the case of quotations embodied in critical reviews and certain other noncommercial uses permitted by copyright law. For permissions, write to the address below.

Robert L. Gard/WGR Publishing/WGR Communications, LLC
619 S. Cochran Ave. #4
Los Angeles, CA 90036
www.distillingrob.com

The author has tried to recreate events, locales and conversations from memories, journals and notes of them. In order to maintain their anonymity in some instances the author may have changed the names of individuals and places. The author may have changed some identifying characteristics and details such as physical properties, chronologies, occupations and locations.

Cover Design: Aaron Trask

Book Layout ©2013 BookDesignTemplates.com

Photos: TriggerChröme Photography by Louis C. Oberlander

Ordering Information:
Quantity sales. Special discounts are available on quantity purchases by corporations, associations, and others. For details, contact the "Special Sales Department" at the address above.

Distilling Rob: Manly Lies and Whisky Truths/Robert L. Gard -- 1st ed.
ISBN 978-0-9896052-0-5 (hardcover)
ISBN 978-0-9896052-1-2 (trade paperback)
ISBN 978-0-9896052-3-6 (ePub)

*To everyone who showed the belief and patience
to help this story see the light of day*

INTRODUCTION

"I should write a book about my life."
Variations of that statement have been spoken to me hundreds of times through the years. Something about me saying, "I'm a writer" sparks strangers to share the personal tale that "everyone" tells them would make for a great book. Parties, grocery stores, weddings, and funerals. America, Asia, Europe or Central America. English as a first language, second or third. The circumstances of these conversations don't matter. People always say they have story to tell.

Not me.

I tell other people's stories. As a journalist I've written more than 2,500 articles. As a screenwriter and television writer I've sold scripts and won awards by seeing the world through eyes that aren't mine. The thought of sharing any part of my life story with any person not in my life never crossed my mind.

When I decided to move to Scotland in 2009, I did so with the intention to write a book. I hadn't written creatively in several years and at that point my life required a resurrection on many levels. A book seemed to be the challenge I needed, though I had no idea what to write. Some weeks after that decision a thought crossed my mind on an otherwise ordinary day in my ordinary work life: use the whisky maturation process as an analogy for how boys mature into men.

I had my escape, I had my idea, and I had my plan. I would use my journalism experience to interview old timers at distilleries throughout Scotland and find out how working in the whisky industry helped to guide them down the path to adulthood. The book was to be an analytical and observational piece. Using industry connections, I reached out to a number of distilleries to set up interviews. All was moving smoothly until I spoke with Jim McEwen of Bruichladdich Distillery on the island of Islay, where I planned to live.

Jim offered me the opportunity to work at Bruichladdich for part of my stay on Islay. Suddenly, instead of being an observer of the whisky world, I was thrust into the heart of it. As much as I tried to stick with my intended goal of interviewing other people in order to examine the maturation theme, the situation quickly made clear the path I had to take: I couldn't stand outside and tell the story I'd intended. I had to be inside the story.

Distilling Rob: Manly Lies and Whisky Truths tells that tale. There is an adage in storytelling that says, "Never let the truth stand in the way of a good story." In this case, I'm flipping that adage around to say, "Never let a good story stand in the way of the truth." The whisky making and maturation process is at times brutal and unsightly. It is also beautiful and redemptive. For me to match the analogy I had to choose personal stories that would hold their own in that comparison. I couldn't let the strength of the theme intimidate me into hiding the truths of my life experiences. I had to hold nothing back, and I hope that I have done so with fairness and honesty.

Despite truth being paramount to this story, I have chosen to change the names of many people in the book. My position is that people chose to be in my life, but not in my story. There are a few instances where the names remained real because the person involved is so well-known or so easily Googled that to change the name is pointless. In some cases, the people involved are so far in the past or on such a periphery to the story that I'm not sure if I have created aliases for them or if my supposed aliases are their actual names. And, in one case, the person's nickname was so appropriate that no other option was available.

The stories recounted here are from my memories of the moments. Perhaps other people have different perspectives of incidents or conversations that are ten, twenty or thirty years old. I've tried to be as accurate as possible to my perceptions of those times. The experiences on Islay are captured as fully as possible in the moment. In many cases, the "present day" dialogue from Islay that is repeated in *Distilling Rob* was written down as it happened or immediately after.

*

There are several people to thank for this project coming to fruition. The first and foremost are my Kickstarter backers, nearly 150 people in all. Their belief in this project and desire to follow this written journey are the sole reasons this story is in your hands today. I may be the teller of tales, but I stand upon their shoulders so that the rest of you can hear me.

My dear friend Linda was instrumental in starting me down this road. Always the firm voice of practical reason, I turned to Linda for advice when I first thought of quitting my job to move to Scotland to write a book. I fully expected her words to wipe this silliness from my mind. Instead, her belief was so fervent that I gained new strength in my decision. In fact, every friend I talked to after Linda was equally supportive, and for that I am grateful.

Tremendous thanks to Jim McEwen, Duncan McGillivray and everyone else at Bruichladdich. They embraced me, taught me and trusted me. I hope I have returned that trust with my impressions of life on Islay and at the distillery. Much gratitude is given to the Fletcher family whose family cottage served as my base away from the distillery and as my writing sanctuary. A very special thank you to Islay-based whisky writer and chef Martine Nouet who quickly embraced me as a friend. She welcomed me into her home on many occasions so I could use the internet (and enjoy her dizzying selection of whiskies).

Greg and Francie graciously gave me the space I needed, both physically and mentally, to finish the first draft of this manuscript while staying at their hostel in Olomouc, Czech Republic. I'm indebted to my old friend Mike for allowing me to live in his uninhabited flat overlooking the Mediterranean in Italy while I wrote the second draft. My travel inspiration Kirsten let me live rent-free at her home in Southern California while I finished draft number three.

Additional thanks are in order for my friends Sunil, Jim, and Amy. Each is an excellent writer in their own right and their feedback on early drafts of my manuscript was immeasurably helpful. Peter Frykholm has helped to tame my tendency to wander with my writing for many years and his copy editing helped to shape this story. Naomi Long's proofreading further refined the final draft.

There are many other people to thank including everyone in the "Whisky Fabric" who has embraced my "writing beyond the liquid"; my longtime writing mentor and inspiration John Herman Shaner; Jen, who helped me to find my writing voice and so much more; Lan and Veria who have no clue how they helped me decide to write this book, but those brief encoun-

Distilling Rob: Manly Lies and Whisky Truths

ters were instrumental; John Shors, a creative writing peer from college whose tremendous success as an author encouraged me to delve into this world once again; and Matt Forbeck, another friend and writer who helped guide me through the successful Kickstarter campaign.

Finally, huge thanks go to my family, my parents in particular. I had a difficult birth and things just went downhill from there. They've put up with me through countless follies, school expulsions, ridiculous decisions and spontaneous life detours. Hopefully they're not finished with loving/tolerating me, because I'm sure there is plenty more unpredictability in front of me.

Thank you to old friends, new readers and anyone else who helped put these words on these pages. Now, go enjoy *Distilling Rob*.

ONE

PROLOGUE

Whisky isn't a manly drink. The monks who invented the spirit called it *uisge beatha* – "the water of life." They could have called it "that which makes the roof thatching go crooked when you've had too much." Instead, they associated it with the gift of life. With a woman's gift.

Water is one of Scotch whisky's three ingredients, the other two being grain and yeast, and it's a very feminine form of water at that. It comes from bubbling brooks, soft streams, and springs that cry from the ground. No raging sea or that preeminent male aquatic role model, Old Man River, here.

This water descends from the heavens and caresses the earth as the Scottish countryside's carved angles unite rain droplets into small streams. The water perfumes itself as it flows through hills of heather, fields of amber grain, rosy bogs and radiant wildflower meadows. Heather, Amber, Rose and Flower – the best nature-inspired names men can come up with are Rocky, Bull and Duckie.

Delicate flavors collected along the journey penetrate the water's DNA as it makes its way to a Scotch whisky distillery to merge with barley taken from Mother Earth. Yeast is added to the barley-infused water, and the new liquid rapidly increases its alcohol content. When these three basic elements finish their time together, you're left with a new liquid that tastes of sugar and spice and all that is nice. The building blocks of whisky.

Everything about whisky is feminine. There isn't a hint of maleness when the distilled spirit comes off the production line. How then has whisky become embraced by men, as seen in centuries of battlefield flasks, smoking room crystal tumblers, strip club plastic cups and sports bar shot glasses? The answer is found half a world away from Scotland's distilleries.

In the forests of America and continental Europe, towering trees rise from saplings to become kings of the wild. Oaks stand sturdy and powerful, reaching tall from the earth, trying to kiss the sky. Eventually, the trees are felled; their wood is hewn, tempered by fire and shaped by force into a cask. The new form is rocked, rolled and bounced. The cask stands empty and purposeless, waiting for fulfillment. Strong on the outside; vacant on the inside. All the image of toughness; all the substance of nothingness.

Something happens to that vivacious whisky when it meets the stoic timber of the empty cask. Something wondrous.

The feminine whisky that went into the cask gives birth. The fizzy fruitiness of the pre-spirit liquid becomes refined and strong. It reaches into the solid oak and releases long-trapped gentle essences of vanilla and honey. The whisky is transmogrified from being purely feminine to embracing the masculine, and the wooden cask has opened its tough core to return the elements needed to round out the whisky. The wood and the whisky unite. They give rise to an individual drink that after years of maturing ventures into the world strong and delicate; placed in a bottle to proudly display its

Distilling Rob: Manly Lies and Whisky Truths

own meaningful character. It's not feminine; it's not masculine. The whisky is simply complete.

How that transformation occurs can be discussed in terms of chemical processes, moonshine folklore, marketing catch-phrases and Robert Burns' poetry. But, this story isn't about whisky. This story is about me, sitting alone on an island off the coast of Scotland, surrounded by eight whisky distilleries.

Some guy in his late thirties, trapped between childhood and the unknown, wondering if I still have time to develop the character and strength I need to transform into a complete adult. A man.

TWO

NEW SPIRIT

Dots of people and matchbox-sized cars zip around downtown Los Angeles, which unfolds hundreds of feet below the twenty-third-floor office where I stand. My forehead forces itself against the clear half-inch of glass that holds me back from the space beyond. I don't know how long I stare down, but slowly a thought sneaks into my skull: "If I go through that window, in less than five seconds I will hit the ground." I lean harder and hear the glass creak. "Five seconds, five seconds, five seconds..." I mutter.

This isn't my office. I usually sit in a cubicle just outside of here; a worker ant in a maze of cubicles that weave their way throughout this floor and the entire thirty-story headquarters of the Los Angeles Unified School District. This office has been empty since I was hired almost a year ago as a strategic communications consultant to help the district promote its multibillion-dollar school construction program. The office was promised to me when I was offered the position, but like so much else with this job, the expectations and the reality failed to congeal – both in the workplace and within me.

Nearly invisible eyes look back at me from the window. Suspended above the faceless people below is a reflection that has seen each step and stumble that has led me to this moment. I absorb the details of the image as we become wrapped up in a reflective staredown, each one trying to understand the other. I see deepening lines on the forehead that weren't there a few years ago; hair that has gotten finer with each passing birthday; and scars of a lost teen battle against oily skin. I look through the faintly hazel eyes watching me, unsure if I'm seeing an old boy, a young man or something in between. Whoever he is, he shouldn't be here.

    Like many people from Los Angeles, I'm not from Los Angeles. I was raised in Beloit, Wisconsin – a working class town where cracked streets were lined with average homes that did their best to smile through peeling paint and cluttered porches. The reek from the riverfront ironworks and cheese factories at the center of town permeated much of the city, giving the air a heavy and biting feel. There were three bars for every church and three churches for every foreign car. Most folks drove vehicles made at the local GM or Chrysler plants – the cars often tinged with rust and the drivers often tapped with beer. Dozens of green parks hosted impassioned Little League and soccer games when the weather was warm. They stood barren and uninviting during the long winter months, their skeletal trees serving as taunting reminders that the things that might make one happy in this town were fleeting. Many locals dreamed of an exciting life elsewhere, but instead spent their lives half-heartedly talking about the routine they surrendered to here.

    Little Robby Gard was yanked into this yawning town with a pair of forceps during a difficult delivery on a hot July day more than thirty years ago. I was named Robert Leslie after two grandfathers: my dad's father – an eighth-grade-educated farm boy who grew up to become an unpredictable alcoholic, and my mom's father – a hyperkinetic amateur inventor with little emotional availability for his kids. I was born into a lineage that historically accomplished little more than having more generations born into it. Well, somewhere about three hundred years earlier was a woman whose progeny evolved into the Kennedys, the Bushes and famous actors and writers. We were the branch that didn't climb up Capitol Hill; we stumbled down from the Kentucky hills, moonshine in hand.

When distant relation Gregory Peck was winning an Oscar for *To Kill a Mockingbird*, my grandfather was killing deer to feed his family. While the Bush presidents had to deal with oil problems in the Middle East, my family scrambled to fix oil leaks coming from cars that were flat-out "used," not "pre-owned." Kennedy cousins made national news with drunken sexual advances. My cousins barely made local news with theft, assault and even murder.

At first glance, I was that cute little towheaded boy whose hair elderly strangers liked to tousle. But, their hands quickly retreated when they saw my massive buckteeth chipmunking over a receded jaw, deathly pale skin barely clinging to a skull that seemed to want to rip through, and eyes sunken so deep that one wondered if my eyeballs were even plugged into their sockets. People say the adult me looks vaguely like Russell Crowe. In my mind, I still look like that undead child from every 1970s horror movie, except I never could whistle through these buckteeth, let alone hauntingly.

I was shy, awkward, insecure, misunderstood. And far from angelic. When I was six I prayed to Satan on Christmas Eve to bring me a toy as a way to hedge my bets in case Santa didn't deliver. My second grade teacher grew tired of me "hiding" in the large trash bin in the back of the room and paid me a dollar a day to stop disrupting class. I raked in the cash until Mom started questioning how I always had money for new *Star Wars* toys and put a halt to the payola scheme. As a preteen I broke into neighborhood homes, though only to rearrange furniture and move pictures. An interior design fetish, I suppose.

Throughout my childhood, I would sit quietly with my parents watching TV night after night, forgetting where I was, who was in the room with me, and transporting myself into worlds where people were confident and didn't have to act out with crazy behaviors to have others notice them, as I did. Our family houses changed with move after move, my parents gave me one brother and then another, new schools, new faces, but the escape of TV and movies remained constant. Promises of a life far away from Wisconsin.

And now, all these years later, twenty-three stories above LA, I look past my reflection and confront the Hollywood Sign I dreamed of seeing one day as a child, pushing through the smog in the hills west of downtown. The trail from Beloit to here has engraved me with more scars than just the ones on my face. The rest are in my heart and now, in this office, seemingly cutting all the way into what's left of my spirit.

This job opportunity came my way some months earlier and for the first time in my life I'd made a career choice based on my future. My adult future - 401k, health, dental and vision. I was making more than a hundred grand and gaining national recognition as an expert in my field. I was well on my way to a highly profitable and high-profile, lifelong career.

It was everything a man could ask for, and I desperately needed the validation the job seemed to offer me.

My job gave me that same sense of meaning, of being someone, that I'd felt the first time I wasn't picked last for the recess kickball game; when I was finally able to stand in front of high school classmates and give a presentation without feeling faint; when I nervously signed my name to a lease after college, even if it was for a shabby apartment; and, most meaningful, when I saw a redheaded woman walk into a crowded room and discovered my shaking voice had the words to make her smile and make her stay; when I touched her hand morning after morning with my eyes still closed, knowing it was the only place in the universe I wanted to be.

I haven't felt that redheaded woman's hand in mine for more than a year, since I'd planned to put a ring on it. Instead, Katie left me shattered and alone, taking with her the bandages she had used to bound together a lifetime of my fears and insecurities. When she was with me, I believed my life was finally centered and had purpose, despite the grueling clashes and struggles that punctured the laughs and the quiet embraces. Those feelings of worth are long gone. All I have left to give me any kind of identity is this job.

And I seem hell-bent on destroying even that.

A few minutes ago, I sat small in a large chair in the office next door – the biggest office on the floor. Across from me, behind a desk that seemed bigger than my cubicle, was the school district's building program director. Harry Donovan is a retired Navy Seabee officer who has helped transform the division from a bureaucratic nightmare that bled millions of dollars into crevasses of mismanagement, to the largest and most successful school building program in the country.

Harry is a genuinely kind, even-tempered and methodically intelligent man who uses those skills to navigate the treacherous waters of politics, unions and media. I respect him tremendously and was honored when he hired me to spearhead the communications and strategic partnership aspect of the division's "green schools" program. He also tapped me to create the public presentations and speaking remarks he gave about the building program.

It's in that latter role that I sit across from him now. Shrink across from him is more accurate. He is twenty minutes from departing for an important presentation before a Los Angeles City Council committee. His PowerPoint presentation is supposed to highlight the program's successes and lay out a persuasive argument for the city to expand their partnerships with us. I've been working on the presentation for the past week.

"Well?" he asks again, clearing his throat with a slight cough. He always clears his throat when he gets nervous, and his mini-coughs have increased exponentially in the two minutes since I entered his office to go over the presentation.

"I, um..." My throat catches as I swallow dryly. Harry's nerves make his throat jittery; my nerves force my throat to close on itself and suffocate the anxious body in which it resides.

Harry takes an obvious and elongated glance at his watch.

"I don't have the updated figures," I finally answer in response to his question about statistics that detail the expansion of community partnerships in relation to the addition of newly constructed schools.

"Did you get in touch with Peter?" he asks, referring to the only person who has those figures. "Like I asked you to do an hour ago?"

"I didn't get a hold of him," I answer truthfully. Of course, the truthful reason as to why I didn't get hold of Peter is because I hadn't actually tried to get in touch with him.

"Did you call him?" he asks unexpectedly. I feel all the blood drain from my face, which tells him what my semantic subterfuge didn't.

I look at Harry with the same terrified eyes that had fallen under my father's glare when I was young. My dad was rarely good at listening to me when I was a child eager to tell him of things I'd done or learned. Instead, he often told me to be quiet and leave him alone because he was busy watching TV. The times I was assured of his undivided attention were when he criticized me for not doing something well enough or spanked me for doing something outright wrong. In most of the latter cases, I'd deliberately misbehave to force him away from the television as my punishment toward him. Or maybe I was looking for his full focus any way I could get it. A way for him to recognize me as me, even if it meant a belt to the backside.

Deliberate failure is something that continues to trip me. Even now, into my thirties, I have a tendency to occasionally, for no reason and with no thought, make preventable mistakes in the face of authority figures. Every time their ire rises, my age falls several decades back to my youth and I quiver in front of them, unable to answer their angry inquiries as to why I screwed up. When I excel at a job, I'm unstoppable, which was why I have built a career that climbed from local Wisconsin reporter to award-winning television writer to Hollywood newspaper editor to national communications strategist. And then I do something to stop myself.

I quietly wait for Harry to explode and yell at me, like bosses in the past, asking how I could possibly fail to execute such a simple task. The verbal smackdown that will snarl I don't belong with the former military studs, construction bad-asses and political ninjas that are my coworkers.

He finally speaks.

"I'll take care of it," he says softly. He tells me I can go, not with anger in his voice, but with disappointment in his eyes.

I leave him as he picks up the phone to make the call I had failed to make. I shuffle past my cubicle and into the vacant office beyond, closing the door behind me. I only stop when my forehead reaches the thin layer of glass between this lifeless room and the frenzied energy of the city below.

I hadn't expected that reaction from Harry, and I hate myself for letting him down. I hate myself even more for letting me down.

I took this job to prove that I could stand tall without Katie there to support me. Even after seeing the woman I wanted to marry walk away and leave me emotionally desolate, I thought that I could at least attain solid life footing in the kind of career your dad brags about to his friends to show he's raised a quality man. Now that illusion is washed away. I thought surviving the gut-churning breakup with Katie a year ago had finally and irreversibly thrust me into full adulthood. The inexplicable little-boy sabotage I just pulled tells me otherwise.

My problem goes deeper than failing Harry. It goes deeper than a lost love – it goes to a lost life. Like a tightly wound spring that is unleashed, I'm whipped by the realization that all the internal political maneuvering the job requires, and the straightjacket of bureaucracy I must wear, aren't helping me grow up – they're binding me into a version of adulthood I've never wanted. This job isn't giving me a chance to find an identity for myself; it's making me dredge up past behaviors as a way to scream through the suffocation. I've had so many struggles in my life that I thought were finally behind me. The awareness they still exist is overwhelming.

Tears fight to break through my eyes and it angers me. The angrier I get the more I want to cry, until I can no longer hold the flow.

"Great, I'm crying at work," I huff to myself. The first flush of anger is washed away by a tidal wave of sadness, exasperation and disbelief.

Distilling Rob: Manly Lies and Whisky Truths

"Why can't I get my life right?" I cry as I push at the window. I don't ask the question for my own reflection; it's a plea to God, someone, anyone to give me an answer. No one does. The emptiness makes my cries sound heavier.

I put my whole weight against the window.

"Five seconds," I mumble again. "Five seconds."

More creaking. How far back will I have to start to get a good running jump through the window? Can I break the glass with a ten-foot start? Would I have to open the office door and start in the hallway? Awkwardly wait for coworkers to smile and pass before I charge into my free fall? This isn't the first time I've thought about ending my life through the years. The loss of Katie had taken me to this brink before, but something pulled me back. Now, I have a foreboding sense that I've exhausted all paths. It's as though thick steel walls are slamming down on the parts of my heart and mind that always seem to discover an elusive escape from a self-inflicted demise. I can't sense the part of my spirit that even cares about my heart and mind. I'm disconnected from my own existence.

Suddenly, from the boundless depths of my being, those steel walls are ripped away with a single word. It swells up from deep inside, lumbers its way through my vocal cords and bounces off the window with an exclamation point.

"D'oh!"

The sound of my voice shakes me away from the glass.

My entire existence is in the balance, and I channel Homer Simpson. I tumble down to the floor and interrupt my uncontrollable crying with unbridled laughing.

"Seriously, Rob? Homer Simpson?" I feel my existence has even less significance than it did a few seconds ago. No visions of Jesus, no wise words of Buddha to pull me back from the brink. I get Homer Simpson. I feel like Jimmy Stewart in *It's a*

Wonderful Life when he finds out the heavenly reject Clarence is his guardian angel.

But there is no other way to put it. I took this job for all the "right" adult reasons: money, image and career path. But, I don't feel any more mature; I only feel like a middle-management bureaucrat. I haven't leaped over the obstacles to adulthood. I've backed myself into a highly paid existential limbo.

"What are we going to do with you, boy?" I ask as I finally get my tears under control.

An image comes to my mind of an island in Scotland that I've known about for years but have never visited. I look upon the skyscrapers, smog, and slow stream of cars, and the idea of a quiet, sparse island gives me a momentary peace. The peace becomes a refuge and in this moment, I decide I'm going to make that refuge a quest.

THREE

JUST LIKE ANY OTHER MAN, ONLY MORE SO

Sitting alone in the rain, clad in my olive drab uniform, gun across my knees, I keep my eyes peeled for an advance squad of enemy troops. Droplets bounce off the pine branches around me, nefariously finding their way down the back of my neck. I shiver with the chill of late November precipitation. I know that as uncomfortable as it is, at least I am well camouflaged. The German troops won't be so lucky. There are two open streets for them to cross and plenty of space between the houses for me to pick them off if they choose to run for cover. With so many tree-lined lots for my firing to come from, they won't be able to find me before I send them back to their maker. I am all but invisible.

"Robby, do you want some chili?"

I whirl in surprise, my gun hitting the ground with a slurp in the mud.

"Mom! I'm busy!" I scream at the short, brown-haired head that barely peeks above the four-foot shrubs. Though I am nine, I'm almost the same height as my mother. Our age difference is nineteen years, but she looks exceedingly young. Most people think she's my slightly older sister.

"Well, I thought you'd be hungry! And the chili could keep you warm, too," she persuades.

I try to argue against her reasoning, but it is pretty cold, and some hot chili, one of Mom's best dishes, does sound perfect. I suppose since I am defending the neighborhood from German attack, though admittedly decades after the war officially ended, it only makes sense for the local peasants to want to help me.

"Fine. But I'm playing."

She reaches through the bushes with the covered bowl she'd brought with her.

"I thought you'd like some crackers and milk, too," she adds, handing them along.

"Thank you," I mumble. "Could you bring me my other gun? It's by the back door. This one is all muddy."

Mom obliges, and I am once again alone, enjoying the meager rations GIs like me have to scrounge for here on the front lines when rain prevents riding a bike to McDonalds.

*

The neighborhood never did suffer an attack from the Germans in the winter or the Japanese or Viet Cong in the summer. My constant patrols kept it safe from foreign occupation. Sure, there were visits from police to haul away this neighbor for beating his wife or that neighbor for dealing drugs. And there were plenty of shouts, screams and door slams that echoed up and down the block. My parents contributed their share of arguments to the neighborhood cacophony. Maybe that's why I was outside protecting everyone from the unseen enemy threat. I was incapable of stopping whatever existed inside the house that scared me.

Dad was twenty-three years old and recently returned from fighting in Vietnam when he married my eighteen-year-old mother. Though neither came from a broken home, their childhood situations were certainly in need of repair. On Dad's side, his alcoholic father would lock himself in the basement for weekend-long drinking binges. Grandpa's father ran out on the family and farm during the Great Depression, making a desperate situation even worse. Another great-grandfather on that side tried to kill himself in front of his family during that same time period.

On Mom's side, a great-great-grandfather did successfully kill himself due to financial hardship in the 1920s. Alcoholism floated about that side of the family as well, which led to additional offences and abandonments. And her father, while not an alcoholic, could be an emotionally cruel man who frequently failed to give his children the attention they needed.

My dad was 6 feet 2, lanky and knew a lot about everything, especially movies. He finished second from the bottom of his graduating high school class, lacking effort, not intelligence. Dad never explained why or how that happened, but each time he met up with friends from high school when I was a kid I could see how hard he tried to be accepted as an equal by them. He had little to say about his life prior to marriage. A story or two would escape now and then, but throughout my childhood I'd only heard a handful of anecdotes. The only father I really knew was the one who disappeared in front of the TV. There were many times he'd play with me for a while, or cheer for me at a sports event, or teach me carpentry, but these fatherly efforts would inevitably fade with him parked in front of the television, losing himself in whatever he could in order to deaden something I wasn't privy to.

Mom lacked my dad's height and natural intellect, though she was smart in an enterprising way. Her 4 feet 11 frame didn't give much of a physical presence, but the constant energy that pulsated from her made up for any vertical challenges. She left college after a semester, coerced by my dad's plea that if she didn't marry him she would never have a happy life. Unlike my dad, she didn't lack for stories to tell, over and over and over. If his silence was a residual effect of trying not to be noticed and beaten by his drunken father, her ceaseless chatter and wandering conversation were remnants of doing anything possible to be noticed by hers. Perhaps that's why she paid so much attention to me and exposed me to as many experiences as possible when I was young; no one had ever shown much interest in her as a child. She didn't want me to suffer the same loneliness.

The tall guy and short gal were as mismatched as could be when they said, "I do." No money. No career prospects. Forced to live with his parents in order to make ends meet. This was my entrée to life on earth as a wedding night "whoops." Dad and Mom had each shifted from being a child to being a spouse to being a parent in a matter of a year. They were learning how to be adults at the same time they were raising a child; getting to know each other while figuring out how to fight diaper rash and ear infections.

My parents were still trying to find who they were as individuals when I was young, which created a volatile relationship. They communicated through clashing, and I was often caught in the middle, running off and hiding when he'd explode with a string of belittling remarks, and she would dredge up his discarded ambitions. I'd let my mind wander to anywhere that wasn't there, pretending to control things beyond my control. Imagining the kids who lived in the big houses on the other side of town, their rooms filled with the most awesome toys and their parents overflowing with perfection.

Distilling Rob: Manly Lies and Whisky Truths

My grandparents didn't leave my dad and mom with an ideal blueprint for how to raise children, so they went on instinct. They understood how their own educational shortcomings had crippled their adult lives, so they scrapped and scraped to send my brothers and me to private religious schools. Despite their best intentions, sometimes the means in which they pushed us into this uncharted educational territory were still rooted in the lessons of their childhoods. You can only teach what you know, and all they knew was what their parents taught them: "hands-on" motivation.

Frequently, I'd climb a tree, sneak onto a roof or crouch in shrubs with a swollen and occasionally bloody behind beneath my military attire: my penalty for falling short in a class or expressing my need for attention at school through some misbehavior. Dad always said I should be grateful that he only used the belt on my bare butt instead of using the buckle, like his father did to him. But I never lived with the pain of Dad's spankings. When I ran outside, those were pains inflicted by the cruel enemy commander whom I had craftily escaped. I was free in my mind's world, not shaking as a helpless young boy in Wisconsin, but adventuring as an unstoppable man in an exotic locale: a real man and not just one of the "guys" like my dad.

For me, real men always had the answers. Their presence always demanded respect. Their looks brought out wild desire and submission in women. They were bigger, stronger and faster. A real man, in my eyes, wasn't any of the males in my extended family, or most of the guys in my hometown. Those guys were just kind of "around." Taking the family to Pizza Hut on Friday nights, going to the hardware store on Saturdays, and nodding off in church on Sundays. Puttering around the yard when sober; punching each other for no reason when they weren't.

The only men that sent my imagination racing were the fictional ones in movies or books. In less than two hours or two hundred pages, people like Han Solo, Indiana Jones, James Bond and the Hardy Boys could save the world and get the girl, or in 007's case, several girls. While my dad struggled to find his place in life, those guys on the screen were solving mysteries, operating on dying people and beating the shit out of the bad guys. As a young boy it was quite the contrast as to what I could do when I grew up: lie on the couch like most grown-ups I knew, trying to forget the menial job I had, or be that on-screen hero.

In the end, I've become neither. I've been like a refugee in a sort of existential *Casablanca*. No home for my maleness. No cause that gives my adulthood definition or meaning. I sit wearily at the bar with the same old cast of sad characters – doubt, trepidation, loneliness and unrealized hope.

I'm not sure if moving to an island off the coast of Scotland is another attempt to escape from the childhood fears and insecurities which still linger in, if not permeate, my adult life, or if it's a bold confrontation of them. I've spent so much of my life running – running out the front door in army clothes to avoid the turmoil inside my childhood home; running inside myself to keep from connecting to others; running toward things bigger and better than me so I could claim confidence by association; running from one job to the next so that I wouldn't have to really stop and think about what is truly important to me. I nearly ran off to the other side of the world once before, when Katie left me broken and alone, just to run.

I am tired of running.

Distilling Rob: Manly Lies and Whisky Truths

Moving to this island will force me to take a stand with and against myself. There is nowhere to run when you're surrounded by water on all sides. And I can't swim to save my life.

The problem with not being able to swim away from an island populated by eight distilleries is the temptation to drown oneself on dry land with whisky. Mom is quite concerned about that very thing when I tell her of my plans. Her horror stories of our family's alcohol and drug problems have scared me from birth.

"Do you know how many alcoholics are in your family history?" she asks when I tell her I'm going to move to a Scottish island renowned for its whisky.

"About 432, plus one if you count Aunt Grace's mouthwash addiction," I answer obnoxiously, incurring an appropriate eye-roll in response.

"It's for your own good," she says in all solemnity. "I'm worried for you. And you haven't gone to church in years. Ever since those liberal elite college professors brainwashed you into ignoring your Christian upbringing."

"Mother..."

"I think what you're doing is great! You have so many talents that I think going away and taking the time to reconnect with God's purpose for you is wonderful. I'm only concerned that Satan is going to tempt you and try to deceive your soul for his own evil reasons."

Mom believes she has an uncanny way of seeing the devil's secret lurking places that the less faithful of us can't notice. I don't have the heart to tell her that the attempt to retrace my life's steps to see how I missed the trail to becoming a man will begin with my blue-collar upbringing, taking me straight to the enemy stronghold of my family's liquid lineage.

I am going to actually *work* at a whisky distillery.

I am something of an expert on whiskey (or whisky as the Scots spell it).

As a newspaper editor in Hollywood, I'd received invitations to everything from movie award shows to private art auctions, new club openings to VIP concerts. One day, an invitation to a whisky expo in San Francisco passed my desk. I jumped at the chance to go. My first lesson in whisky at that expo came at the hands of a representative of a Scotch distillery. He patiently walked me through the subtleties, and I was hooked.

Something about whisky touched me. It was an outsider. Elite people could effuse about wine in an exclusionary manner. Popular people in their designer jeans and little black dresses could flit about Hollywood parties with their various vodka concoctions and vacant conversations. Working folks had their beer, and then another, and another, while watching elite athletes on TV or reading about those Hollywood parties in *People*. Whisky, on the other hand, was a mysterious drink. That kid in class who always seems like he has a secret, but no one talks to him to find out what it is.

Bogart drank whisky when the clues in the case seemed just out of reach and the woman he wanted even further away. Robert Johnson wrote the blues late at night with a bottle by his side. Writers and whisky, well, the list is endless. Wine begs for conversation, vodka for parties, and beer for sports. Whisky...well, whisky asks you to stay home within yourself, to look at where you are and figure out how you ended up here.

Following my recovery from that day slumped in sobs on the office floor, I thought about options for my escape from LA. And the one that kept flashing like a lighthouse beacon was the island of Islay (pronounced *eye-luh*), off the coast of

Distilling Rob: Manly Lies and Whisky Truths

Scotland. Alone with my thoughts, like Bogart. A chance to reach into my heart and pull out whatever mess was in there, like Robert Johnson.

Eight whisky distilleries have made the island something of a mythical land in the minds of Scotch drinkers around the world. I'd written about several of the distilleries through the years and grown especially attached to an icon in the industry: Jim McEwan. He is part of a team that resurrected the closed Bruichladdich (pronounced *brook-laddie*) Distillery and made it into an international innovator. I'd talk to Jim about Islay at industry events and noticed there was a flickering twinkle in his voice when he described what it was like to live on the island. The notes I took in those interviews were all business, but the tone behind the words spoken to me was almost like a siren call. Jim was one of the first people I contacted with my impulsive idea to move to Islay, and without any prompting, he presented me with the chance to work at Bruichladdich. I accepted before the words were out of his mouth.

After ten years in LA, three of which have been spent sitting in traffic, I want something radically different. From my earliest childhood memories, I always wanted to run from the working-class world into which I was born. I did, and I haven't stopped. I have a feeling that if I am going to find the life answers I'm looking for, I need to jump back into the world I leapt from, even if it's on the other side of the planet, and take a fresh look at my roots and at me. Though, in the realm of blue-collar jobs, working at a whisky distillery *is* pretty damn sweet.

*

Downtown Los Angeles disappears behind me for the last time as I begin my journey, my quest. I'm in the first few miles of a cross-country trip to Wisconsin where I'm to leave my car at my parents' house before heading overseas. In the rearview mirror I see the rising sunlight dab the city's icons: Staples Center sports and concert arena, the modernist Aon Center, and the sky-scraping U.S. Bank Tower. I can barely make out LAUSD's headquarters cramped among them, where I had pressed against a window two months earlier, wanting to tumble through.

    The bulk of my material life is crammed into a 10x10 storage unit within drive-by shooting range of the Santa Monica Freeway. The value of my Italian shoes alone could finance my journey to Scotland. They are some of the many things I couldn't survive without in LA, crammed in a box beneath my contemporary photography pieces, which are leaning against my Danish mid-century modern tables: all the hints of luxury that I'm leaving. Now, my most vital possessions are a toss-up between the waterproof boots that will keep my feet dry on the water world I'm moving to and the six pairs of underwear that will cover my butt for the foreseeable future.

    Most of the people I'm leaving behind are asleep this early on a Saturday morning – the incredibly successful friends who know nothing of the shy and insecure working-class boy inside me; the movie stars who inspired me to leave home only to stun me with their shortcomings when I finally met them; the bosses I'd let down, the girls I'd pick up, and the pick-up hockey opponents who knocked me over.

    Katie is also out there somewhere, and I try to fight the intruding image of someone else's arms wrapped around her. I'm leaving much behind as the white lines dash past my car, but her absence travels with me.

    I'm certain I'm not leaving LA because of Katie. I'm doing this for me: neither a boy nor a man, just an uncertain human being who is stepping into darkness to see what I can find.

FOUR

THE GRAY ISLAND

The ferry's rust-dappled hull grinds to a slow stop against a creaking wooden pier that wears seagull droppings like a pox. The splatters are brilliant and bright beneath the heavy grayness that presses down on the dark cliffs enclosing the harbor. Three buildings with fading whitewash hint at humanity, but the port seems uninhabited, aside from a sputtering bus and a few vehicles.

I retrieve my luggage and anxiously wait with the other passengers for the gangplank to pull level with the ship. My fellow travelers are natives to this whisky-making island, not strangers like me. They fumble for car keys or make phone calls to let folks know the ferry has arrived. I stand solitary and go over my instructions for the three hundredth time since we set sail: get on the bus at the ferry terminal and request the driver to drop me off at Persabus Road. This is requiring a major mental readjustment of my concept of public transportation.

In the U.S., you get off at the designated stop, no ifs, ands or buts – and that's if you actually ride public transportation. Now I've been told I need to ask the bus driver to drop me off at a road whose name I can't even pronounce. Is he going to give me that "bloody spoiled American" look? I think to myself,

"What happens if he tells me he's not allowed to do that?" To begin with, I've no idea where I'm going. And the gray mist is starting to get heavier. If there is miscommunication and I end up stuck wandering alone in the rain...

My mind slowly pushes me to decades earlier – to Wisconsin when I was just four years old.

*

Another silent morning at preschool has ended. The silence is self-imposed. In my four years of living in a volatile home, I've learned it's wisest to remain quiet and out of sight. I try to save the teachers and other kids the effort of ignoring me by not being noticed. On this day, however, as the last of the children are being driven off by their parents, I am approached by a preschool aide who sees me standing alone in the school courtyard.

"Where's your mom?" she asks, and I shrug according to my code of silence. "Were you supposed to get a ride home with Joey?"

Joey is my neighbor and my only friend at the preschool. I occasionally catch rides to and from preschool with his mother, whose outdated beehive hairdo frightens me. In all honesty, I can't remember if I was supposed to get a ride with him today or not. On some days, my now-sober grandpa picks me up, but I know today isn't one of those days. The third ride option is my perpetually tardy mom, who is nowhere to be seen, and preschool ended more than half an hour earlier.

"Yes. I think Joey is taking me home," I finally whisper, though I'm not certain of my own words.

"Well, Joey's mom already left," the aide half-sighs. "I'll take you home."

I hesitate for a moment and gaze desperately for my mom, but the aide's annoyed look sparks me into a shamed shuffle to her car. I climb into the aide's front seat (the common way to travel before child seat laws) and we depart.

We drive down Beloit's main street, which hasn't changed much in one hundred years, and I watch as workers from nearby factories stumble out of several bars as their lunch breaks end. We cross the bridge that spans the Rock River, which divides the middle-class east side from the working-class west side of town, where my family lives. I sit tall and peer down to the river to see if I can catch a glimpse of the rats that perpetually scurry on the banks alongside the cheese factory.

As we turn down my street, the aide hurriedly rolls up her car window and remarks about the dark summer storm clouds that swirl above us. She pulls to a stop in front of the house that I silently point out.

I run out of her car as fast as I can, with hardly a goodbye, as I'm scared that I've been such an intrusion on her life. The car pulls away as I reach the huge oak door, which I'm still not big enough to open on my own. I'm about to knock on the door when I feel my face go numb. I turn around and look at the side of the house. Mom's car isn't in the driveway. She must be trying to pick me up from preschool.

Frantically, I drop the finger painting I made today and reach for the door handle. I know my parents never lock the door. The sky flashes and rumbles angrily as the wind starts to push against me. The handle successfully twists and I push as hard as I can. The heavy door doesn't move. Again, I push, shove, implore the door to open. Not a single movement. I think about how effortlessly my dad opens the door. The handle disappears in his hand and the door eases open under his command. I try to picture myself bigger, stronger, and try once again. I'm meaningless to this door.

The dark sky unleashes a torrent. Immediately, my own tears join the flow. I watch as the finger painting I'd made of Mom and me at the park disintegrates at my feet, the colors dripping away from the front porch and disappearing toward the street. All I can do is stand and shudder, weakly calling out, "Mommy...Mommy...Mommy..."

*

"Excuse me," the passenger behind me says in a Scottish inflection. I am blocking the gangplank, awash in my own thoughts. I quickly move aside, worried that I'm already giving locals a reason to disdain me and I haven't even set foot on the island.

I hurry off the ferry and scurry to the bus as a light rain starts falling; a four-year-old boy hidden in the body of a man thirty years his senior. If the bus doesn't drop me off at the right place, I'm going to be standing in this rain totally alone, crying "Mommy" all over again.

*

The bus pulls away, abandoning me at the end of a long single-track lane. The driver's stony stare after I asked for the fourth time if this was Persabus Road told me we'd reached the right spot. The bus speeds off quickly, as though the driver can't leave me behind fast enough. I feel the stares of the other riders through the bus windows as I stumble into the rain, encumbered by my belongings. Their unblinking eyes disappear as the bus taillights fade behind the spray of water kicking up from where its wheels meet the rough road.

To my right is a hilly field with half a dozen shaggy highland cattle alternately eyeing me and chewing grass. I examine the rickety fence that serves as a feeble barrier between the mammoth-like creatures and me. I pray these aren't the kind of animals that easily anger and charge, because the thin, warped wood of this fence couldn't stop an annoyed cat, let alone a half-ton beast.

In front of me is a road that rises over an uneven hill and disappears into the bleak horizon. The driver assured me the cottage I seek is down there. Somewhere.

The rain comes down harder and the wind blows me off balance. I pull the hood of my waterproof jacket over my head and march on, my guitar case whipping haphazardly in the wind. It's minutes past three and already the January daylight is fading. Islay shares the same latitude as Siberia, and I feel as isolated as a gulag prisoner.

After walking for somewhere between ten minutes and an hour, I see a solitary farmhouse ahead of me. This is the first sign of life I've seen since being stared off the bus, though the house's darkened windows make me wonder whether it's a home for people or for wraiths. I peer further down the road and see nothing but high hills, thin streams and distant forests. I pray this farm is my destination, though I can't detect the separate cottage I'm to rent anywhere. At this point, I'll stay overnight in the barn if it means getting out of the rain, which has mocked and defeated my waterproof attire.

Chickens scatter out of my way as I cut across the farmyard to the dark house. I reach the front door to find a rain-soaked note still barely attached. Most of the ink has run off, but I can make out the words: "cottage" and "unlocked."

"What cottage?" I plead to the note. This is all I need: getting soaked on a doorstep with another disintegrating piece of paper in my hand. I'm on the verge of crying "Mommy" when I decide to walk around the side of the house. I spot the cottage.

I feel like I've stepped back in time a century. Or five. Sandwiched between the worn stone remains of two four-hundred-year-old farm structures is a brightly whitewashed two-story building. It's in wonderful condition and looks as though it was put up yesterday and that yesterday was 1685.

I momentarily forget about the rain as I take a slow turn around the cottage. I'm careful to avoid strewn pieces of farm equipment, some appearing to have rusted in place hundreds of years earlier. Looking from the front of the cottage toward the direction I just came, I see a long sweep of brooding forests and brown fields that slope to the sea.

Around back is the un-whitewashed evidence of this cottage's age. My new home shares a stone wall with one of the ruined farm structures. Hills rise sharply behind the cottage and continue climbing into the distance. Sheep are scattered among the slopes, and behind a worn split-wood fence immediately next to the cottage are a grazing horse and its pony pal. Perched atop one of the closer knolls appears to be the remains of an ancient chapel, roofless and ominous through the sheets of rain, made eerier by a connected, crumbling graveyard.

I walk to the cottage's front door and try the handle. Unlocked, as the note promised. Thank God I'm a lot stronger than I was at age four. I successfully open the door. I take one last look around before my dripping self and waterlogged belongings enter. There were hundreds of people who lived on my street in Los Angeles. The apartment buildings were so tightly packed that whenever someone became amorous with their windows open their energetic sighs rebounded off the adjacent buildings in "round" fashion; but, instead of "row, row, row your boat" it was more like, "moan, moan, moan, oh god."

The only moaning I hear now is that of the wind. I wanted something different from LA. I have it.

Distilling Rob: Manly Lies and Whisky Truths

"What the hell have I done?" I say to a passing chicken, which pays me no heed.

I cross the threshold.

FIVE

THE BALL DROPS

Islay is a dualistic island. The day is divided into two: dark and not-quite-as-dark. The sky is either raining or starting to rain. The fields and hills have either sheep or sheep shit in them. The people work on farms and the supporting trades, or are part of the whisky industry and associated tourism. They are either Gaelic speakers with family roots going back hundreds, if not thousands of years, or they are newer transplants with mainly English roots. Legend has it that the island itself was once two bodies separated by a shallow inlet, but at some point in the last few thousand years an isthmus connected the two. The name Islay may be derived from the Gaelic I-Leach, meaning island-half.

Some 150 years ago, nearly twenty thousand people lived on the island. Today, the population is a tenth of that. Disease and hardship destroyed lives and drove people away in the mid-to-late nineteenth century. Those that remained have clung to life through one of the only viable means of financial subsistence available to them: making whisky.

If I ever need a reminder of which country this island belongs to, all I have to do is look down. My living room carpet is tartan. There are three shades of blue-green in it that meld darkly into the traditional Scottish pattern and give me the illusion of walking on a layer of viscous dish soap. The carpet isn't particularly plush and the stone floor beneath it emits a constant chill. Consequently, I keep the room's small stove perpetually on to chase away the chill. I say "on" because it's a twenty-first century electric version of what once was a traditional stove. In the days before electricity this stove would have been alight with a mixture of wood, coal and peat – dead vegetation that has compacted for thousands of years in bogs and is harvested to heat homes and to add smoky aromas to whisky.

Three mismatched couches are crammed in the living room, along with a small TV and several side tables. Theoretically, the TV receives a hundred channels, but the constant wind and rain pounding the satellite dish leaves me with more static than sitcoms. I've added to the clutter by dragging a small dining table into the room to serve as a desk. I could have easily set up my computer and work area in the kitchen, but the tile in that room lets the cold stone foundation throb through even more than in the living room. At least in here, I have the heating source to keep me warm.

Hanging on the walls are uncomplicated watercolor paintings of local sites that manage to pick up the blues in the carpet. The impressionistic images are the closest I've gotten to the beaches, distilleries and historic ruins they feature. Most of my first week here has been spent settling in and adjusting to the time change. With only six hours of daylight, and most of that darkened with ever-present rain clouds, I haven't been able to get out much and explore.

Two doors that lead outside stand on opposite sides of the living room. The front door opens to the farmhouse courtyard. A small tree, perhaps no more than five feet tall, is immediately outside the front door. My heart stutters almost every time I walk by the tree because its tangled branches are home to a terrifying avian. The farm has half a dozen truly free-range chickens that wander as they please – except for one. The day after I moved in, this lone brown-feathered, red-eyed *gallus domesticus* took to perching in the tree, and it has yet to move from its roost. To paraphrase Edgar Allan Poe, the chicken is never flitting, still sitting, with eyes of a demon that is dreaming, overseeing my every move through the front door window.

The back door lacks chickens, ravens and all other sinister flying frights, but beyond it lies an undeveloped expanse of hills and bogs – at least in the present. Hundreds of years ago, islanders built a chapel and cemetery a quarter mile away from the present-day cottage, both of which are now the kind of ruins that bode ill in Gothic literature. However, I'm not too concerned about ghouls sneaking into my cottage at the stroke of midnight; I'm convinced my devil-spawn chicken-stalker is so creepy that even the undead don't want to come anywhere near it.

The highlight of my time in the cottage so far has been to play Goldilocks. I have my pick of three upstairs bedrooms and was alternating between them to find the one that feels just right. Last night, I made my final decision and chose the one that has the only bed with more mattress than springs. There is no closet or wardrobe space whatsoever in the cottage, so I use the two spare bedrooms to store my clothes. With four shirts, three pairs of pants and not enough socks or undergarments to last me a week it may seem a bit odd to use two entire spare bedrooms as closets. But I do it anyway. Because I can.

I plop down on one of the living room couches, nearly sinking to the floor. I speculate the owners took the springs out of it and stuck them into the poking mattresses upstairs. I squirm my way into a less uncomfortable position and reach for the cuppa I've made – black tea. I look around at my modest new home. It has none of the interior design elements I'm used to in LA. No custom furniture. No paintings by buzz-generating artists. No blindingly large plasma screen. This is a homey dwelling, lovingly put together by average people that wouldn't be out of place in Beloit, aside from that tartan carpet.

Twenty-some years ago I was in a living room very much like this in my hometown and like now, it was a time where my psyche and my life were frantically in flux. I lean back on the couch, close my eyes, and open my memory.

*

New Year's Eve and I'm fifteen. It's an age where staying up to watch the ball drop on Dick Clark's Rockin' New Year's Eve doesn't give me the sense of accomplishment it did just a couple of years ago. I'm too young to hang out with friends for the midnight transition, not that I have more than a handful. So, I spend the evening with the only option available to me: I'm babysitting two young neighbor girls.

Their parents are with mine at a church party for a safe, alcohol-free evening to welcome another year. The church gives my parents the direction and meaning their lives didn't have when they were practically children raising children of their own. Their deep faith has inspired Mom to open our town's only Christian bookstore. Church has softened and given strength to Dad, who has desperately needed it this past year.

His rock-bottom high school graduation ranking was a testament to his rough childhood, not to his brains. But, the lack of formal education and inability to follow through on person-

Distilling Rob: Manly Lies and Whisky Truths

al and professional commitments haunted him time and time again. Earlier in the year, he'd lost yet another office job – whether through downsizing or his own fault, I don't recall. For the past few months, he's been working a second shift factory job, operating a machine.

Factories are a way of life in my hometown, and most people who work in them can't imagine anything better than a union job. Factory work gives them enough money for a house, maybe a fishing boat, plenty of brews at the bar and pays for their kids' hockey equipment. My dad is miserable in this world. Yet, he does it without complaint. He has a wife and three boys to feed, and house payments to make. He is trapped, but unlike his grandfather, doesn't abandon his family to find a cowardly way out.

He and the neighbors are desperately enjoying the break away from their working lives tonight. I'm simply glad to be out of the house. I've just tucked the girls in for the evening, and Dick Clark is on in the background, though I'm not paying much attention. I lie down on a couch and take a slow, careful look around the living room, the centerpiece of the small brick home that was built in the 1940s when wartime factory work was booming. The TV sits on an old trunk, which is in better shape than the trunk next to the couch that doubles as a coffee table. Both undoubtedly contain board games, blankets and bible devotion books.

Two side tables are on either side of the couch, with a third side table next to the La-Z-Boy recliner, which has stuffing peaking through worn upholstery. Each table has a lamp, all mismatched and secondhand, emanating dull yellow light from too-low wattage bulbs. The obligatory "Footprints in the Sand" poem hangs in a frame near the TV. Chipped freestanding wall shelves hold crosses, plastic praying-hand sculptures and Precious Moment figurines. The shag carpet is twenty years older than anything else in the living room, aside from the couch, which can't hide its age despite its newly crocheted quilt.

All across my hometown are thousands of houses exactly like this. Our own home, though ranch and not brick, mirrors the religious kitsch interior design.

"One day, I am going to have a home like this. Two girls to tuck in. Lie down and watch TV," I think with increasing unease. "Then I'll have to get up the next day and do it again. And again. And again..."

My mind, my body seizes at the thought. I try to get up, but I can't.

My chest hurts. Collapses. Into my lungs. I pant desperately for breath. My heart tries to rip its way out from the excruciating pressure.

The room spins, lifts, closes, flies, teeters, plunges into my head. Dick Clark sounds distant, the other-side-of-the-galaxy distant. I smell the aroma of years of deathly routine trapped in the couch, carpet and chair. My stomach churns bile and I want to vomit, but I'm too light-headed to even open my mouth. I can no longer breathe. The joylessly smiling Precious Moments figurines are knowingly watching me die.

I see Dad's anesthetized face as he walks out the door for another second shift at the factory. I see myself dying with that same look.

I roll off the couch onto the worn shag. Like a fighter at the tail end of a ten-count, I force my way to my wobbly knees. The room is still shaking and unstable. My chest feels the weight of this home's unspoken despair. I collapse backwards against a chair and force air into my constricted lungs.

I focus on a family portrait above the couch. A weary husband, a wife too young to look that old, and two gap-toothed girls born to have this very life for their own one day. They are all smiling, but the specters of future frowns haunt those smiles.

"No," I say, not as a plea, but as an affirmation.

Blood creeps back into my face, my chest lifts slightly and I can feel the slightest wisps of air creeping down my throat.

*

Nearly twenty-five years have passed since that living room led me down the path to this temporary island home. Pinpointing precise moments that lead to life changes is a murky exercise, often shifting with age and time. But that New Year's Eve night most definitely marked a cutting turn for my young life.

A week later, I returned to school for the second semester of my sophomore year. I had a new haircut. I wore different clothes. Instead of a quiet presence in the back of the classroom, I sat up front and made comments. I told jokes at lunch. I even talked to girls. Well, said hello to them is more accurate, but even that was huge for me. Three months later, I ran for class president, giving a speech in front of people I hadn't spoken to in more than a year and a half in school with them. I won.

I had no clue how to break out of my boyhood insecurities, no concept of what I needed to be as an adult. All I knew was that the life I was born into was going to kill me. And I had to change that.

SIX

EAT, PREY, DRINK

I feel like a mime doing a wind-walking routine as I trudge the fifteen minutes to the rural bus stop closest to my cottage. The effect comes easily at the moment, as nature's fury is pitching sixty-miles-an-hour wind my way. I can literally lean into the wind with all my weight and not fall over, which is no small task for 190 pounds. I fear a gust will pick me up at any moment and carry me away, dropping me into the icy gray waters of the North Sea where I will disappear forever.

Three weeks since my arrival and I've developed a desperately needed routine that structures my island life. Next week, I'll leave the cottage indefinitely to start work at the distillery, which will require embracing an entirely different schedule. For now, this routine helps pull my mind from the encroaching loneliness that presses against me in the isolated cottage. I sometimes go three or four days without seeing another person. Living exclusively in my own relentless presence is not what my distraught mind imagined in that office all those months ago. The dream of an island was a two-dimensional one, but now that I live it surrounded by all the shapes, contours and shadows of reality, I devour my twice-weekly reprieve from solitary confinement.

Tuesdays and Saturdays are my bus days. The bus takes me to Bowmore, one of the three main villages on Islay, for groceries – the sustenance of my stomach, and Internet access – the sustenance of my sanity. Bowmore, which is twenty miles from my cottage, has a population of perhaps eight hundred, most of which live in whitewashed eighteenth century buildings situated along a sea loch. The village and its streets follow the curve of the shoreline up to the small hills that look down upon the Bowmore whisky distillery.

My bus stop is at the beginning of the line that runs from the north side of the island to the south side, where it ends at the Ardbeg distillery some thirty-five miles away. As always, I am the first person to reach the bus-stop shelter, which is little more than a Plexiglas hut full of graffiti and trash. I am surprised that I am the first one here today because my fellow regular riders come from the other direction and have this gale blowing at their backs to launch them here at twice their normal walking speed. Finally, I see the first person edge out from a doorway among of the small gathering of homes near the stop.

Ellie is clad in a red woolen jacket that clings to her small frame, even in this wind. Her short salt-and-pepper hair holds up formidably against the gusts. She's the cook for a little family restaurant in Bowmore, bestowing each soup, shepherd's pie and pastry with a matronly heartiness. We greet each other with a casual "Hiya" when she enters the shelter, and she takes a disinterested look at the sheep in the field behind us.

Liam is next up. The retired lorry driver always appears as though he's just woken, looked out the window, seen the bus coming, and stumbled to meet it. Today is no different. His worn synthetic winter jacket is only partially buttoned, and even those don't line up. One shoe is securely tied and the other...is from a completely different pair of shoes. At least they're both in the same color scheme. He gives a half-hearted wave and in one fluid movement his hand descends from the wave into his pocket, emerges with a cigarette and meets the lighter that magically appears in his other hand. He takes a deep drag and exhales the smoke into the small bus shelter, rather than out the front opening. Liam apologizes for filling the shelter with smoke, and I would take that apology a bit more to heart if he didn't repeat this same act and apology every single time he rides the bus.

Two regulars down and one to go. And here comes our fourth musketeer with his tweed cap-topped head, a frayed blue blazer beneath a too-large overcoat and a gnomish shuffle that pushes him to the shelter. If one of the "little people," the faerie-folk of Gaelic mythology, ever had a human embodiment, it is my fellow bus rider. Rudie is somewhere between 70 and 120 years old; yet his twinkling eyes dance about like a toddler. I know his ruddy cheeks have tales to tell, but in three weeks my ears have yet to penetrate his accent. Every day, he takes the bus into town, waits for everyone else to get off, and then hobbles his way to a seaside pub. He parks himself in a corner and orders a pint, quietly reliving a thousand past conversations while he gaily watches a smattering of other patrons, and when they're not around, observes seabirds fishing near the shore.

As always, Rudie reaches the shelter at the same time as the bus, which shudders to a stop. We assume our boarding order so naturally that airlines could learn from our system. Ellie moves to the front; it's ladies first, after all. I step behind her as Liam crushes out his cigarette and helps Rudie into position in front of him. There are only four bus drivers on Islay, and today we have Callum, the least talkative of the bunch. He is also the driver who dropped me off in the rain when I arrived on Islay. Every time I board a bus he drives, his eyes seem to say, "You're still here?"

Ellie strides aboard with another curt "Hiya." I follow and fumble a little less with my coins today than I have been, as my ability to attach a UK denomination to a coin size continues to improve. Rudie is up next, helped by Liam to his seat behind the driver. I move to the center of the bus, where the windows seem to be a touch cleaner. This gives me a nice view of the drive into Bowmore, where I can glimpse vast moorlands, sheep-strewn hills, rugged coastal cliffs, primeval forests and pristine beaches that ebb into the ocean.

My view is disrupted shortly after we depart by a pounding hailstorm that whacks the bus with ice pellets. The high wind amplifies their impact. Still, Callum doesn't alter his driving. I've learned that no matter what the weather, no one here alters their driving habits. It doesn't concern me, even as we rapidly take the sharp curve around the old chapel outside of the hamlet of Ballygrant – which consists of a row of cottage homes, an inn and three small shops. I go with the flow as Callum's bus does a slight fishtail past a farm and screeches to a halt to pick up another rider.

The hailstorm passes by the time we reach the co-op grocery store in Bowmore. The co-op is the center of life on this side of the island. It's a place where neighbors say hello, schoolmates catch up, and the latest gossip is exchanged. I bypass the co-op for now and head to the Lochside Inn, a restaurant/pub/hotel that overlooks the Loch Indaal, a sea lake. I need to take care of my Internet activity before I buy my perishables, and the Lochside owners let me use their WiFi with the purchase of a pint. Or two.

Distilling Rob: Manly Lies and Whisky Truths

Being from Wisconsin, I am no stranger to pubs. The state has more bars-per-capita than any other state in America. I grew up in the days when adults could bring kids to the bar without lawyers ready to pounce with a lawsuit or so-called i-reporters there to upload mobile photos of juvenile delinquency to CNN. Bars were a place friends and I would play pinball or pool while the dads chatted and had a beer. Or two.

I remember thinking at the time that the discussions they had were so dull. Sports, of course, which was pretty cool. But lawns? Car repairs? The sweaters and blouses Miss O'Brien, my teacher, wore? They always seemed to talk quieter and laugh louder whenever they mentioned her. I was disappointed to imagine that one day I would grow up to have these boring "manly" conversations. Well, once I hit puberty, the sweaters-and-blouses chats didn't seem quite so bad.

The little pub at the Lochside is no different from the ones back home. I walk in and take a seat at a table near the bar. Four middle-aged farmers occupy their usual stools and take up the banner of bar conversations heard 'round the world. First they chat about sports – football – the soccer kind. Next up is the young tart who works at one of the distilleries. Apparently, sweater discussion is big here as well. Finally, they reach the point where the conversation turns to the mundane subjects I yawned at as a boy. Today, it's sheepdogs.

"What good's a dog if he be more scared a'noise than the sheep be?" Hamish says. "You kin take the nip outta a dog, but you kin no put a nip inta 'em."

"Aye." "Aye." "Aye," the other three respond in unison.

"Jimmy McMillan has a stupid sheepdog that'll run straight for a gunshot 'n take the whole flock w'him," Danny inserts.

"Ah, fuck. Jimmy McMillan would a'do the same thin'," Andrew says soberly.

"Aye." "Aye." "Aye," the others chime. They quietly return to their pints, having exhausted that line of conversation.

My steaming fish and chips arrive along with a pint from the local Islay Ales brewery. I attempt to respond to emails as I eat my fried lunch without having too much grease stick to the keyboard, but am losing the oily battle. My friend Yvette has emailed me a video link to a TED talk by Elizabeth Gilbert, author of *Eat, Pray, Love*. When friends heard about my plans to travel, they noted my love of food, readiness to talk to single women and my passion for whisky and dubbed my trip *Eat, Prey, Drink*. I haven't read the book at all, but I figure watching a twenty-minute video of the author will spare my keyboard more gooeyness from my French fries.

Elizabeth's talk is about the nature of genius and the torment that artists often face when they try to live up to expectations of creativity.

I wrote my first fictional story at the age of four – a tale about a turtle that ends up being eaten in a soup. I was dark even then. Through the years I've dabbled with everything from short stories to screenplays, sometimes finding success, but mostly not – either through my own inability to take a story to completion or through rejection from the powers that be regarding publishing or filming a story.

Her talk progresses and I find myself drawn in by her theory that genius doesn't exist fully internally, but is a collaboration with an outside power – God, the universe or pixies – that is trying to work with you to tell a story. She relates her own struggles of not feeling "good enough" with the erratic nature of her creative writing endeavors until one day, she tells that outside force to please stop. Stop jerking her this way and that. Stop filling her up in a flurry and then on a whim leaving her feeling abandoned. She gives that outside force a stern lecture and suggests that they work together, rather than antagonize each other, to best utilize their creative partnership. God agrees.

Her experience strikes me deeply.

I've felt the same way with my own creative efforts, but this is even how I feel about my entire life – like some external force picks me up to carry me higher, but then lets me fall and fail. The emotional audience applauds Elizabeth's bold stance when she describes how she asked to be an equal partner of her creative collaboration with the universe. I find myself swept up in the sentiment of the Web clip and I unexpectedly and inexplicably start to drip tears. I want what she's achieved – a partnership with her purpose and passion, but I don't solely want it for my creativity, I want it for my life. I want to scream "stop!" to this rollercoaster of uncertainty and inconsistency. I want to collaborate with the world, the universe, to live as best I can as a man and as a person.

The video stops and everything is quiet. I mean *everything* is quiet. I look toward the bar through watery eyes. The four farmers stare at me with suspicion, beers warily held at their sides as though my sniffles are a threat to their manhood. A temporary awkwardness fills the space.

"So, you say that tart was wearin' a skirt the other night?" Hamish asks as he raises the beer to his lips and turns to Danny.

"Aye, an' a short one if it was anythin'."

I drop my head in my hands and start laughing to myself. I asked for collaboration with a higher power and I received tears. Is this a sign I'm stuck forever on my own, or is it the beginning of a beautiful friendship?

SEVEN

YOU CAN'T HANDLE THE TRUTH

It's Friday the 13th and the lights have gone out at the cottage.

Let me repeat and expand. It's Friday the 13th and a hauntingly violent storm has ripped electricity from the island, plunging my four-hundred-year-old cottage into utter darkness as I sit alone on the edge of the Scottish moors with the crumbled remains of a fourteenth century church and graveyard frighteningly close to my back door.

As much as I extol fiction as being the guiding force for my youthful impressions of manhood, I also curse it for being the lifelong bane of my nightmares. Horror flicks and supernatural thrillers have terrified me since I accidentally came across *Rosemary's Baby* while flipping through the channels when I was five. Unlike many childhood fears that fade with age, my terror of the supernatural never lessened.

I read *Dracula* in college while alone in a dormitory, and slept for a week with a bulb of garlic and a wooden stake I'd fashioned within reach. Seriously. When a girlfriend forced me to see, *The Ring*, I spent half the film with my head hidden in her lap. I didn't turn on my TV for four days after. Then there was the real-life ghost experience I had while staying at an eight-hundred-year-old Irish manor a few years ago:

I was awakened at 2:00 a.m. by the spoken-word intro to a song on my iPod. I had drifted off while listening to music to distract my brain from the stories the lord of the manor had told me during a post-dinner-drinks conversation (which included a few heavy pours of the Bushmills Millennium bottling) that centered on the estate's otherworldly residents. My heart nearly stopped when the song intro woke me, as I was certain it was the whispering words of a ghost. Once I gathered my bearings I laughed to myself and mumbled, "If a ghost really wanted to scare me, he'd just have to kill my iPod and leave me in deathly silence." In an instant, the device, which was plugged into an outlet, lost all power. I stopped breathing. I turned on a light to find that the electricity wasn't out and that the iPod was still plugged in. By all earthly deduction, the music should have still played. It didn't, despite my best efforts to restart, reboot and resurrect the iPod. I spent the rest of the night cowering under my covers, finally getting up at dawn to find that the heavy wooden shutters of the room's only window were barred shut from the inside – something that I deliberately hadn't done the night before for fear of being trapped in the room with a ghost. Let's just say if I'd been any whiter when the owners saw me stagger to breakfast, I would've been as translucent as my nighttime visitor.

At present, the wind howls like a banshee, rain lashes the windows and doors like fingernails trying to claw through the glass, and a cold chill envelops me. Thankfully, the latter is because the heat has gone out and not because apparitions whirl about me, though I'm sure they're on the way from the nearby graveyard, as memories of the Irish manor haunt my thoughts.

Distilling Rob: Manly Lies and Whisky Truths

I stumble and fumble my way to the kitchen, where I've seen a flashlight and candles. Luckily, I remember where they are stored and soon have light. I peer out the kitchen window to see if the main farmhouse is also without power. It isn't there. Nothing is outside but abyssal blackness.

Within minutes, I have eerie shadows flickering off the walls, their darkness mirroring the light cast from my candles. The only power I have is on my smartphone, and I've relayed my dilemma to my Facebook status page. Helpful friends immediately offer important advice: "Don't sprint outside in your underwear." "Don't answer the phone." And, "Don't run upstairs with your top off and your breasts flopping about." My friend Paulette provides the most immediately implementable advice: "Keep sipping Scotch and everything will be all right." Then my phone signal disappears.

I think about all my fictional heroes and can easily picture each of them confidently sipping whisky in this situation, waiting for the menace to approach. Bogart would have that world-weary, "I don't give a damn about demons, that dame already sent my heart to hell" look on his face. Bond would exude sexual energy, expecting a gorgeous succubus to fly in through the fireplace to try to destroy his soul. He would lustily bang her before dispatching her. Indiana Jones, well, this happens to him all the time.

I pour a dram of 15-year-old Bruichladdich, which is from the very distillery where I am to start work on Monday. The whisky's aroma rises to my nose as pleasant honey and fruit notes. I slowly ease the spirit through my lips, and nutty and malt flavors mingle on my tongue to make me forget about the spirits in the room. My mouth is warmed by the rich liquid that spices its way down my throat. Paulette is right. A little Scotch does keep the monsters away.

I look around the barely lit room. Once again, it reminds me of that living room from long ago, where my teenage anxiety attack put me on a path to leave the working-class life to my family and friends. I can hardly believe that I'm back in a similar room and in two days will be immersed in manual labor when I start work at the distillery. In the years between being a boy who wanted to escape blue-collar Beloit and now, I've had ample opportunity to view my family and peers from youth from a different perspective. I now see many of them as men who have something I don't. Their lives, as unspectacular as they may seem from the outside in terms of wild tales and adventurous anecdotes, appear to be moving forward with family and work, and not floundering like my single and now-unemployed life is. Many friends who never left the region where I grew up have a kind of contentment I didn't achieve with all my running. They're comfortable and happy in their world, aren't they? Or am I romanticizing their lives in the same way I idealistically imagined the lives of movie stars to be when I was growing up?

When I was a newspaper editor in Hollywood I had plenty of interactions with the silver-screen heroes from my youth. And, I quickly found they really weren't all I expected them to be.

*

"Excuse me, sir," drawls a husky voice I'd first heard when I was a quarter of my thirty-two years. The man slides by me to occupy the empty seat on my right. I am in Malibu for the opening night premiere of a new play by John Herman Shaner, my writing mentor and friend. In his youth, John heard the same siren call I did and moved to Hollywood to be among his heroes back in the 1950s. He went on to a successful Oscar-nominated writing career. His best friend from those early

Distilling Rob: Manly Lies and Whisky Truths

years also had a bit of success in Hollywood and at this moment is taking a seat next to me.

The audience is filled with dozens of actors and actresses I'd watched living larger-than-life on screen. None of them are bigger than the sunglassed superstar that slides past me. I'd seen him act crazy, act brave, act tough, act cruel and act compassionately. From the stories John told me, this joker could still go out any night of the week and come home with a girl, or two, or three, a third his age.

"Certainly, Mr. Nicholson," I say, as I pull my knees tighter against the seat for him to pass than is possible for me to do for a non-Oscar winner.

"Thank you very much," he offers. His act of sitting has more strut than most men's walks.

The curtain rises and it is apparent that everyone in the audience, even the other reasonably well-known actors, watches Jack with invisible eyes, so palpable is his presence. Early in the play, John's protagonist makes a humorous reference to Jack Nicholson that causes eighty heads to whip around to see the actor's response. His is the only audible laugh, as we non-superstars defer our reactions to him. Everyone quickly follows with chuckles of our own. I am at an angle to glimpse the eyes behind the sunglasses. There seems to be a resignation to the reality of fame.

Halfway through the show, the main couple – a recognizable actor and actress in their mid-fifties – has an intense argument. They stomp back and forth across the stage, raising the dramatic tension as their voices clash. Suddenly, in the midst of a passionate speech, the actress collapses in a heap. A strange pall falls over the audience. This is an oddly dramatic stage moment that doesn't make sense for the scene. The actor stops cold in his tracks and then quickly walks to his co-star.

He kneels at her side. There is a cough from the third row. Hushed whispers start to rise as the actress doesn't. The actor turns to the audience, trembling.

"Is there a doctor?" he murmurs feebly.

The whispers stop.

"Is there a doctor?" he pleads with desperation.

I quickly look around. The guy in the front row had stopped a team of Russian spies in a 1960s TV show. The woman in the row behind him had been a savvy and sporty detective in a 1980s series. I take in more faces: that guy fought aliens; this one saved his farm from evil developers; there's that actress who was a nurse in an army hospital. None of them make a move. I look to Jack. He's undertaken every heroic act imaginable in his films. He is as paralyzed as me: a guy who has taught first aid and CPR.

Finally, a man jumps up and jogs to the stage. He is nobody, in Hollywood terms. Just as he reaches the actress, she shakes with a start, her eyes flying open. She sits up, blinking in a daze.

"What happened?"

We soon find out the actress fainted due to not eating all day because she was dealing with opening night nerves.

There is a collective exhalation from the audience. I notice Jack nervously fiddling with his hands. His helpless hands.

I'd been in LA for several years when this incident happened. My newspaper role took me to hundreds of celebrity-filled events. Seeing my heroes in their natural element, where their physical and personal peccadilloes had eroded my idealized vision of them was one thing. Witnessing them behave exactly as me, with a total inability to act in a potentially life-and-death situation, knocked the final leg off the pedestal where my role models had stood for so long.

Distilling Rob: Manly Lies and Whisky Truths

In my years in Los Angeles I'd spent time with attorneys worth tens of millions of dollars who behaved no differently than entitled children; politicians who were so personally fragile that they had to bandage their egos by subjugating those beneath them; and billionaire business giants who had to subtly and not-so-subtly display their wealth in order to see their own worth reflected back upon them. Now, the men and women behind my fictional heroes were also all too human.

*

The lights pop back on as power is restored to the cottage. The shadows cast by the candles disappear under the incandescent glow of four lamps. This room reminds me of the living room where I had my New Year's Eve panic attack and revelation years ago. It doesn't matter, though. I am different.

I am here not because I have failed and am falling into my blue-collar upbringing. I am here because I need to go back to the beginning, the basics, to figure out why my life journey left me wandering and wondering. And what better way to start than with the three elements of whisky: barley, yeast and water, the building blocks of the water of life. I can't wait to get to work at the distillery Monday because I need a new foundation, a new building block, for my life.

EIGHT

DEPARTURES

The bus crew is lined up again this morning. Only this time there is less room in the shelter. I have my 4800-cubic-inch backpack sitting by my side and my guitar slung over my shoulder. As part of my distillery initiation, Bruichladdich management has offered to let me stay in their on-site guesthouse for a few weeks. I'll be one of several people there, but it allows me to immerse myself totally in distillery life.

Ellie offers her regular "Hiya," with a slightly raised eyebrow. Liam realizes my backpack doesn't allow him enough room to blow smoke into the shelter, so he stands well-outside in obvious frustration. Rudie takes a long, shaky look at me and shares a wizened, inspirational anecdote. I think. I still can't understand a word he says. We board the bus and I can sense Liam trying to peer into the small opening at the top of my backpack to see what mysteries it holds. The crew departs in Bowmore with each person giving me a curious look to see if I will follow them off the bus. I don't. I stay on for the additional thirty-minute drive to Bruichladdich. No one else steps aboard. It's only me and silent Cal as my chauffeur.

Callum takes the only route to Bruichladdich, around Loch Indaal. I see the village of Bruichladdich and distillery across the bay as soon as we leave Bowmore, but we have two wetlands, a pub and market, sheep herds and a prehistoric standing stone to pass before the slow road around the loch reaches my destination.

The long ride gives me ample time to think about the upcoming distillery job, but I decide not to dwell upon what will happen. I lean against the side of the seat and feel the cold stickiness of my head pressed against the dirty bus window. Twenty years ago an equally dirty bus took me away from my hometown for my long-dreamed-of escape from the familiar and uninspiring streets. Rather than being a moment of elation, that departure took me in an unexpected emotional direction.

*

I had come a marathon-distance since that New Year's Eve panic attack two years earlier. At least it seemed that way to everyone who knew me. I was student body president. Star of the high school musical. Volunteering to work with underprivileged kids. My parents were proud and teachers were enthusiastically supportive. I was popular and played that popularity well, but I couldn't even look at myself in the mirror. The moon-crater face probably had something to do with that.

My success and popularity didn't come with all the amenities, either. I didn't date at all through high school. I later found out that my best friend Mike wondered if I was gay, because I wouldn't even talk about girls. Sure, I'd make comments about movie stars (*Sports Illustrated*'s voluptuous swimsuit-issue pictures on my locker door nearly had the nuns slap a suspension on me) but I never verbalized the unrequited aches and agonies I had for the girls in my world as I watched them hold hands and make out with my friends. The closest I came to attempting a date was posting signs for an essay contest where the winning girl would get to go to homecoming with me. It was as passive-aggressive as imaginable. But, I thought that maybe one of the girls I pined for would write about her hidden feelings for me and...well, you can guess where that went.

Like a reprieve from the dating guillotine, I eventually had a girl who pardoned my ineptitude and expressed interest in me. It took everyone and their mother – literally, someone's mother – to get me to ask her to our senior prom. I did, and she enthusiastically agreed, which left me speechless because this wasn't any girl. It was Sabrina, the most beautiful and lovely girl in the entire school. We had been casual friends for a couple of years, but I never even allowed myself to imagine anything was possible beyond that. This was Beauty and the Acne-Beast.

I had no idea how to date, despite her best attempts to train me in the weeks leading up to prom. We spent plenty of time hanging out, going to movies and out for pizza. Every other guy on the planet wouldn't be able to keep his hands *off* the most beautiful girl in the school. I couldn't even figure out how to put my hands *on* her. She growled in frustration at the end of each date because nothing romantic came close to happening. I had no idea what the problem was. I was picturing prom as being like the season-ending episode of a TV series where the guy and girl finally seal everything with a kiss. No reason to rush the cliffhanger, right? Right...

Sabrina had reached her frustration apex by the time prom rolled around. After the dance was over, she made sure to ply me with enough champagne at the senior after-party that I couldn't resist being wrapped in her arms. Still, I insisted on rolling out all the dramatic lines I'd been practicing for weeks in anticipation of the big night. So, my prom make-out session went something like this:

"Thank you...for everything," she says, thrusting her tongue in my mouth.

"Let your mind go and let your body follow," I slur mindfully as I pull away from her body.

"Right," she says, jerking me back toward her long-neglected lips.

"I don't know what tomorrow will bring, but tonight all that matters is here and now," I whisper dramatically as I fight to stay away from her lips long enough to get my line out.

She pulls away. "Oh...please don't sound so gay." Back to the lips.

"Sabrina," I say as I roll her over – and right on top of two friends who are trying to sleep next to us through our clumsy passion.

"Get away from me!" says a friend, shoving us away. I roll Sabrina the other direction, trying to dodge her darting tongue so I can bring out my biggest dramatic statement of the night.

"Sabrina," I start again, staring into her eyes dramatically. "In two weeks we graduate..."

"Will you just shut up, already? Shut up, shut up, shut up!" she demands. Her eyes leave no room for another line from me.

I stop speaking and nod like a little boy who does what he's told, and I spend the rest of the night doing just that.

We all know how people who never have good things happen to them handle life when something finally goes their way. I was essentially like one of those bingo-playing, trailer-living, chain-smoking, beer-drinking, motorized-shopping-cart-riding folks who win a $100 million lottery. I fell apart. If I didn't know what to do before the big night, then I was certainly in no man's land in the days after prom. I was the clueless Inspector Clouseau of romance, bumbling at my every needy and nerdy turn. When her interest in me waned and disappeared within a week of prom, I was confused, lost and abandoned. I took the only route of comfort I could: I turned to my role models of music and film. The guy sitting on the dock of the bay that's got nothing to live for and nothing's coming his way. The guy that moves to Casablanca to get as far away from Paris as possible.

I bought a Greyhound bus ticket to Colorado.

My parents had known for years about my desire to leave Beloit. Phrases like, "I'm going to leave here and never come back," left little room for misinterpretation. Being voted "Most Likely to Leave Beloit and Never Return" in high school only added to the inevitability. They weren't surprised when I applied to and was accepted by Colorado College, one of the best liberal arts schools in the country. I was to move there in August. My demolished love life accelerated that Rocky Mountain departure by two months. I didn't think about what that would do to my parents – their oldest child leaving the nest abruptly. I didn't think about what that would do to my friendships – no last summer of fun together. All I knew is I was crying myself to sleep at night with a heart that had finally glimpsed something beautiful only to have the door slammed shut.

A week after graduation, and less than three weeks after the one moment of romantic happiness of my teenaged life, I'm at our local Greyhound bus terminal. A suitcase and a backpack lay on the ground in front of my feet like a bridge. I look down at the $79 one-way ticket gripped crunchily in my hand. My parents and brothers are gathered around me. I'm as unyieldingly numb as a soldier getting loaded on a transport for battle. Everything is moving fast and slow, blurred and sharp.

Dad looks down the street, stoically unengaged, toward the factory where he works. As much as my looking up to fictional characters has led me to this dramatic departure, so too has my reality: years of not feeling worthy enough to be noticed by my own father. Now I stand here next to Dad as he stares at the town he never left and I stare at the ticket that will hopefully never see me return. Silent strangers.

He tried to speak with me this morning, in his own way. I came out of the shower to find a sheet of lined yellow paper neatly folded on my bedroom dresser. I opened it and recognized his elegant handwriting. He'd never written anything to me before, aside from a signature to the birthday cards Mom bought. I glanced at the paper with clenched teeth, closed thoughts and rising anger. How dare he try to communicate with me now, right as I'm going out in the world on my own! I sneered at words like "proud of you," "quite a young man" and "love you very much." I crumpled the paper and threw it into a wastebasket with the sole thought of, "Too late." That coldness only emphasizes the newfound position as my own man that he can't control. I am off to start my own new life, brokenhearted, but bold.

A large, beat-up bus pulls to a creaking and dusty stop. Jeff, the mellow teenaged brother who is often lost in his own world, nonchalantly looks at the bus as though he sees someone off on an hourly basis. Greg, though only nine, is the emotive, verbose voice in the family.

"There it is. The ride to the rest of your life," he says with the gravity of a family patriarch.

"Oh, honey, don't say that. You don't want to make him scared," Mom says in her June Cleaver way, which doesn't hide her own fear. I don't dwell on her nervousness though. I'm still mad at her for trying to sneak a small travel ironing board with a pink floral cover into my suitcase this morning. Just what I need to show all the guys when I start college in the fall.

Distilling Rob: Manly Lies and Whisky Truths

I peer into the bus windows at the other passengers, who have been gathered from throughout the Midwest. They startle me. To a person, they look empty. I thought everyone who rode a cross-country bus was on a life adventure toward freedom like me. These people look like they're heading toward the life I'm leaving. Or maybe that is their life, no matter where they are or where they're going.

My legs move like dream legs, heavy and thick. Dad picks up my backpack as I drag my suitcase to the baggage compartment. The gruff driver slides both in with hardly a notice of me. I was expecting a gregarious man who would regale me with road tales, and we'd be best friends by the time we reached Nebraska. Instead, he wearily tears my ticket in half.

No one gets off the bus. This town isn't a place people come to. A handful of other people I don't recognize are getting on the bus, sharing emotional and in some cases, overwrought farewells with their families. Not my family.

"Bye," Jeff says, getting straight to the point, as usual, and we quickly embrace.

"Good luck. You should be really excited. Enjoy college in the fall, make sure to study hard. Your future depends on it," Greg says and I cut him off with a hug before he slips into a full-blown soliloquy.

Mom reaches up to hug me. I'm a full fourteen-inches taller than she and at seventeen, only a year younger than she was when she married. I think this crosses her mind as I sense sniffles through her hug. She pulls away from me and looks at me with glistening eyes.

"Rob, I want you to know..."

"Yes?"

"It's OK to pick at blackheads, so they don't become zits, but don't pick at whiteheads or zits because they will leave scars. And you don't need any more scars."

"What????"

"I thought you should know that."

"And you choose now to tell me?!?"

"It was on my mind."

"Oh good lord, woman! You say the stupidest things at the stupidest times!" Dad seethes with his usual brusqueness toward her.

"I'm sorry," Mom replies with her typical half-hearted submission to him.

Dad shakes his head and mutters. He shakes my hand and gives me a hug.

"Take care, bud. Call us when you get there."

He holds the hug unusually long and uncomfortably tight. For a moment, my heart flashes open and I think about mentioning his letter. I don't.

I march up the bus stairs and walk haltingly down the aisle. I find a window seat and look out at my family. My life. The only life I've ever known. My safety. My shelter and sustenance. My brothers, my built-in companions. I take the quickest look imaginable at the rest of the passengers and return my gaze to the family. Tears streak down Mom's face. Dad stands with his jaw clenched in determination. Jeff and Greg look simply sad.

What the hell am I doing? I am on a bus full of weird strangers! My life is out there! The bus jerks forward. I hold a weak hand to the window as my family gets smaller. I take a staccato breath that holds back the sobs that want to come out. I feel exactly like I did that day in preschool, standing in the rain alone and unsheltered, separated from the warmth of my home.

I quickly shield my face from the other passengers so they won't see my emotion.

I haven't even reached the city limits and already I feel more like I am part of a family than I'd felt in the years before I'd boarded the bus. But, there is no turning back, and the trip is just starting.

*

"Here ya be!" Callum says a second time, loud enough to get my attention. I return to present-day Scotland.

The bus is stopped. Out the window stands a courtyard of 150-year-old white buildings. A long line of casks painted blue-green spell out the distillery's name: BRUICHLADDICH. I gather my backpack and guitar and shuffle out into the light rain. Callum pulls away, leaving me standing in the rain, alone and unsheltered. The trip is just starting.

NINE

HELLO LADDIE

Karl is five years older than I and lives in the yellow ranch house on the other side of the street. It is sandwiched between the red ranch house and the brown ranch house, which is directly opposite our white ranch house. For the past two summers, Karl has been my best friend, despite him being in his early teens. He is my Army partner on many important missions, like launching smoke bombs at the old plastics manufacturing plant that lay in the nearby woods or sneaking up on the ever-sleeping security guard at the local history museum and firing caps at him.

After one of these missions, we return to Karl's house for our usual round of lemonade. His older brother Kirk – the ever-mischievous Kirk – is in the kitchen when we walk through the back screen door. Kirk takes one good look at us, fully dressed in our military garb with our little guns, and starts laughing in a way that makes me feel less gallant than I'd been a few moments earlier.

"Whoa!" he says, holding his hands up. "Is this a stickup?"

Karl throws a plastic hand grenade at Kirk, hitting him in the head. The two tussle for a minute, laughing the entire time.

"I need to pee," Karl says to no one in particular. He points to me and speaks to Kirk as he heads to the bathroom, "Get Robby a drink, will you?"

"Shuuuuure," Kirk responds with a grin. "What'll it be, GI Joe?"

"Lemonade," I squeak.

"Nah, you've been out fighting all day, right?"

I nod.

"You need a man's drink."

I am horrified at the prospect of having a man's drink. All I can think of is coffee. I hate coffee. It must be ninety degrees outside. Please, God, don't let him give me coffee! Kirk quickly eases my fear.

"Nah, it's nothing bad. It's like coke, but from a bottle, not a can. I'll even give you some ice, OK?"

Ice is the magically cooling word I need to hear.

"Yes, please!"

He reaches into a cabinet above the sink and pulls out a huge bottle with a white label. The liquid inside is brown.

"See, just like coke!" he assures me.

This brown elixir of men is poured over ice in a small glass. Kirk hands me the glass.

"Here you go, soldier! Drink up!"

I greedily oblige at the same moment Karl re-enters the room. Though he is ten feet away, the spray of bourbon whiskey from my mouth hits him with enough velocity that he doesn't have time to cover his eyes.

*

That was my first introduction to the world of whisky, that manliest of manly drinks. Not an auspicious occasion, I'd say. But, one that stuck with me. I wonder what Karl and Kirk would think if they could see me now as I enter the grounds of an actual whisky distillery.

Italy has cathedrals. India has temples. America has malls. And China has a big-ass wall. Scotland? Well, its finest engineers put their brains together a couple of centuries ago and designed the Industrial Age's grand interpretation of the one-thousand-year-old art of whisky making. Gone were the small huts and caves that housed the illicit pot-sized stills that produced illegal hooch for the local village. In their place were government-sanctioned (and taxed) businesses producing Scotch whisky on a broad consumer scale within the walls of a distillery: a sprawling chalky-white maze of buildings where nature's barley, water and yeast are introduced to each other through the artificial constructs of humans.

Most modern alcohol companies now are like trading cards for multinational corporations. Distilleries, breweries, brands and beverages are swapped regularly between corporate interests when companies are looking to cut losses, consolidate assets or diversify holdings. As a result, you get drinks that are produced for corporate and consumer continuity, not necessarily for quality. Bruichladdich, affectionately known as the Laddie, was formed with a different approach not beholden to the economic whims and production rigidity of other companies.

Corporate decision-making led to the distillery being mothballed in the mid-1990s. In 2001, the man who has given me the chance to work here, Jim McEwan, left his position at a rival multinational whisky company to help purchase and reopen Bruichladdich as an independent distillery. Jim delights in screwing with the preconception of what a whisky should and could be for consumers. As a result, Bruichladdich's whiskies are often wildly different from one another, and certainly unique among Islay whiskies, and their marketing outreach (or grandstanding, as some in the industry would say) is sometimes outrageous, in a cheeky way.

These are the facts about whisky making and Bruichladdich that I've brought with me to Islay. As I step away from the bus and walk toward the distillery gates, those academic thoughts are buried deep in my mind by the reality of the moment. The immediacy of being confronted with a working distillery and the recognition that my tangible interaction with this world is about to begin send my heart racing. I'm not looking at a historical documentation of the Industrial Revolution as my boots crunch on Bruichladdich's cracked pavement; I'm living it.

The distillery's gates are only forty feet from Loch Indaal and a briny sea breeze is quite strong here. The site is at the base of low hills that extend as far as the eye can see, into fields and bogs. I enter a courtyard that is flanked by five whitewashed stone-and-mortar buildings. If not for the handful of cars and trucks parked alongside them, I would be viewing the same picture that drivers of horse-drawn carts would have seen some 150 years ago.

Grainy aromas thicken the air around me, driven through vents atop a pagoda-shaped roof of one of the buildings. Steam drips from the vents and that which isn't carried off by the wind cascades off the three-story pagoda roof. The hot white condensation clouds roll down the side of the building as they creep into the courtyard and infuse my nostrils with the smell of malted barley. I know that within the building, barley is being subjected to hellishly hot water in order to start the first stage of the whisky-making process.

A faint sound of machinery comes from another part of the same two-hundred-foot-long building. My breath catches with excitement as I figure out what the sound indicates – that gleaming copper stills three times my height are being fired up to extract the alcohol needed to make whisky. I can only imagine what Katie would say if she could see the look of awe on my face as I catch a glimpse of the stills through a window. I remember when we went into a whisky shop while on a vacation to London and she patiently and amusedly watched me sample single malts like a kid in a candy store. I can envision her laughing and snapping a picture of me right now as I giddily run up to the window to get a closer look at the stills.

Sadness sweeps the fantasy away as I remember she doesn't know I'm living on this island, doesn't care what excites me or scares me, and probably doesn't consider my life at all now that it's not part of hers. If she does think of me, I don't know if her thoughts are smile-eliciting memories of the beautiful times together or heart-cringing recollections of our worst moments that only reinforce the wisdom of taking a life path that doesn't include me. Most likely, I'm far removed from her mind. That's the advantage of doing the leaving in a relationship: you're not the one whose present life is regularly interrupted by the emotional shrapnel left behind from the end of the bond.

I force my focus back to the moment and continue scanning the courtyard. I see several other buildings that look like a granary, warehouses and a bottling hall. My eyes stop on a small sign attached to the building nearest me. Chipped paint on the sign still forms the word "office" and points to a lone door at the top of a rickety external staircase.

As I climb the staircase, praying it holds its integrity long enough for me to reach the top, I wonder if I'm inspired or underwhelmed by my first view of the distillery. Given Bruichladdich's status as a whisky success story whose bold marketing adventures make it a media darling, I'd expected more than a handful of time-worn buildings and a staircase that looks ready to fall down as I tiptoe up. But, what Bruichladdich lacks in twenty-first century coolness, it makes up for with nineteenth century authenticity.

I enter the office door to find an unheated reception area with a frayed carpet and a couple of mismatched chairs. A sliding-glass window separates the entry area from a side room where a receptionist should sit, but the wires dangling from a black-screened computer monitor and dust-covered piles of paper on the reception desk indicate it's been some time since a person greeted a visitor walking through the door I've just closed.

Minutes pass without any indication of activity from the room beyond the receptionist's desk. I'm nervously eager to see Jim McEwan as soon as possible to find out what he has in mind for me during my time at the distillery. Jim's enthusiasm is what put Islay on my internal map in the first place. I can't wait to sit down with Jim over a few drams and imbibe his wisdom about whisky and life, but all I'm doing is waiting.

Cold wind blows through the cracks in the outside doorframe, making the entry area so chilly I can see my breath. Even as an adult I still have a hard time shaking the Midwestern over-politeness ingrained into my social self. However, the shivering brought on by the cold room forces me to drop convention, forgo my waiting and open an unmarked door opposite the exterior door.

I gingerly walk through the door, afraid of setting off an alarm or getting pounced upon by a Scotsman who is a little too close to his Celtic warrior/Viking invader roots. The only thing greeting me is a blast of warm air, which I eagerly inhale. I've entered into the middle of a hallway that branches to my left and to my right, with a few closed doors along each wing

Distilling Rob: Manly Lies and Whisky Truths

of the corridor. I pivot to shut the door behind me and when I turn back I'm startled to see a petite middle-aged woman standing in front of me. The woman is dressed professionally, with short hair and smart glasses, and offers a genuine smile.

"You must be Rob," she says.

I'm taken aback by her sudden appearance and by her knowing my name. My surprised look only widens her smile.

"Don't worry, dear. I was told by Jim to expect you. My name's Grace, and I'm the office manager," she says in a melodically soothing Scottish accent.

"So, is Jim expecting..."

"I'm afraid Jim's away from Islay attending a whisky conference." The news is entirely unexpected. I feel like Dorothy when she found out the wizard was away from Emerald City.

"Don't worry, dear. We'll take good care of you," she quickly continues in an effort to lift my crestfallen face.

Grace allows me to leave my bags and coat in her office, gives me a cup of hot tea to warm away the chilly remnants of the reception area, and leads me to the office of Duncan McIlvery, the distillery manager. Duncan is in his early fifties, with salt-and-pepper streaks throughout his hair and beard. He has a genuinely kind face and a relaxed, friendly demeanor that is obvious without him even saying a word. He's on the phone when I enter, but he waves to me to sit down in an empty chair next to his desk. I give Grace a "goodbye-for-now smile" and take a seat.

Duncan is apparently speaking to one of Bruichladdich's production team about a fickle generator. His conversation gives me a moment to look around his office. Numerous production charts and sample bottles filled to varying levels with whisky leave no doubt about what he does for a living. But, I'm more intrigued by the personal photos Duncan has hung on the walls and tilted carefully on his filing cabinets. Some show Duncan beaming while restoring what looks to be a small steam-engine-powered cargo boat. Other pictures show him smiling even more deeply while playing with what I assume are his grandchildren. The youngest child, a boy, wears the kind of thick glasses reserved for people with severe vision impairment, and Duncan's biggest smiles appear in photos where he plays with the boy.

Duncan ends his call and reaches across the desk with a firm handshake pulsating through well-weathered hands.

"Welcome, Rob! We're glad to have you working with us for a while. Jim's told me all about you," he says with a gleam.

We chat for a few minutes about what has led our respective paths to cross. I spare the emotional details of my journey, but honestly admit I basically need a change from my life in LA. He tells me that he worked his way up the distillery ladder, like so many people in the industry do, from rolling casks in the warehouse to firing up the stills, to running the daily operations of the entire distillery.

Our conversation ends with him presenting me with a pile of work attire that will be my first uniform since I worked at McDonald's as a teenager. I'm actually kind of excited to be clad in whisky-gear. It's the same excitement I had when I would wear my camouflage clothes while patrolling the neighborhood as a kid. We bid each other farewell. I start to leave his office to retrieve my belongings from Grace and head to the distillery guesthouse to change into my new uniform, but I stop before I reach the door and turn back to Duncan.

"Wait a second; don't you have forms or something for me to fill out?" I ask. I'm working in a factory and can only imagine what the UK equivalent of OSHA paperwork must entail.

Confusion washes over Duncan.

"Forms?"

"You know, emergency instructions, safety regulations and such?"

He pauses before nodding slowly.

"Last week, one of our lads in the warehouse wasn't wearing safety gloves while rolling casks. He lost control and had a finger crushed between the cask and wall. The doctors were able to reattach it," he says.

I jerk my head back in surprise.

"Don't let that happen to you, and I think you'll be all right," he winks.

And with that, I enter the world of whisky.

TEN

OH, LORDY BOY

I am nervous. Really, really nervous. My life's unexpected twists and turns have led me to interview movie stars (with a dry-as-cotton mouth), party with rock stars (praying to God they wouldn't ask how a pasty, non-tattooed thing like me made it backstage), chat with billionaires (whom I feared were secretly cringing at my Midwestern working-class accent) and even ask successful and beautiful women out on dates (albeit with a shaking voice and the very real possibility I would launch the contents of my churning stomach on them before I finished my date request). None of that compares to the type of nerves I feel right now.

Clad in bright blue mechanics overalls and wearing a yellow hard hat, I'm certain I look like a life-size Pez dispenser. My ill-fitting, steel-toed boots thud ominously below me as I precariously grip the slippery metal railing on the slipperier metal stairs. The hard hat digs a crease into my forehead as it tries to cling to my increasingly sweaty head. My first day at the distillery starts where the heart of whisky making begins.

The mash house provides a perfect job for guys like me who took more pleasure in playing with my oatmeal as a kid than I did eating it. In mashing, you take massive amounts of barley and mix it with immense amounts of boiling water.

Drain, store the liquid and do it again, each time trying to extract more of the sugars needed for alcohol production. At Bruichladdich, four of these "washes" garner some thirty-six thousand liters of hot sugar water, called wort, for the fermentation process. That's the technical part.

The cool part is watching and smelling the mashing process happening in front of you, which is what I get to do today. The mash tun is an immense open-air vat where the barley "oatmeal" is mixed with the aid of giant mechanical arms with menacing metal teeth. During each forty-five-minute wash, the steam opens your pores in a way that would have real Beverly Hills housewives begging their husbands to pay big spa bucks. It also makes for these damn slippery stairs.

The mash house is where the primordial ooze that becomes whisky is slowly created. It's also the Big Bang to my genesis as a whisky maker and the return to my working-class roots.

Bruce Springsteen often sings of the working-class man, bringing mournful melody to lives of men who slowly give up living as they find themselves trapped in factory life. I think that would've been me had I stayed in Beloit. I would not have been one of those church-going, little-league-coaching family men who are fulfilled by their working-class family life. I would've been like my grandfather, locking myself away with a bottle in hand, sobering up enough to make it to my next shift and then coming back home to booze. If that kind of working-class man is considered a loser by the educated masses, then I would've been a massive failure.

Fortunately, I failed at being a failure. Unfortunately, that is due in large part to my absolute ineptitude with manual labor tasks. And that is what has me completely nervous at the moment. I'm not merely bad at most manual labor jobs, I am horrible.

Distilling Rob: Manly Lies and Whisky Truths

My first (and only) day as a butcher's helper, I shredded ten feet of sheep's intestine being filled with bratwurst meat, spraying ground pig innards into the furthest reaches of the butcher shop. The first (and only) time I drove a tow truck, I ripped the side mirror off as I pulled into the garage. My day's wages went to replace it.

Frito-Lay, that multinational manufacturer of artificial nutrition, apparently rewrote their employee manual after I worked there for a summer in college on the packaging line. My job was simple: put small bags into big boxes. I lagged well behind my peers on the packaging team, and spent two months on the Cheetos packing line, which was the slowest-moving line and the one which you were supposed to master before moving on to Lays potato chips or Fritos. My languid loading caused considerable problems, as the incoming mid-summer extra hires had no place to train because I was stalled out on the introductory line. Against my deep insistence that I wasn't ready to move up, I was shifted to the potato chip line where the chips didn't have to go through the extra process of having chemical cheese caked to them, as the Cheetos did, which made that line move faster. Much, much faster.

*

My entire body shakes with fearful apprehension as the first bags of potato chips start rolling down the line toward me twice as fast as Cheetos. I stand paralyzed as my potato chip Pamplona thunders ahead relentlessly like a herd of bulls. Boxes fill up as quickly as my hands can transfer bags of chips into them. *Still, the bags come.* The pretty coworker I have a crush on, who previously hasn't acknowledged my existence, sees the looming danger I face and momentarily leaves her packing line to toss her extra boxes my way to save me time from constructing my own. *Still, the bags come.* I give a panicked glance to LaVerne, the packaging line manager who is an Isabella Sanford look-alike. She shakes her head like Mrs. Jefferson would do at one of George Jefferson's screw-ups and walks away. *Still, the bags come.*

I picture Lucy Ricardo stuck in a situation like this where the candy assembly line overwhelms her. Lucy ate some of the candies to stave off the attack. I have no such option. *Still, the bags come.* My packing table is breached. The bags spill over and fall at my feet with a crinkly crash. *More bags come.* I am up to my ankles. *More bags.* Shins. *More bags.* Knees.

"Oh, Lordy boy, you is sad, sad, sad!" LaVerne says, as she finally stops the assembly line from sending more waves of Lays my way. "You lucky this your last week, 'cause I ain't seen nothin' like this 'fore. You need one those retard jobs."

A friend told me that the next summer, the employee manual mandated that new hires had two weeks to master Cheetos, or they would be fired. Who says an individual can't have an impact on the operations of a giant corporation?

*

I make it to the top of the stairs without sliding back down. My first minute of work hasn't been a failure. Yet I am convinced that despite my safety-first attitude, some ill will befall me.

I have the most absurd imagination when it comes to situations like these. I watch the teeth of the mash tun's mechanical arm methodically grind its way through the grist gruel. I picture accidentally dropping my hard hat over the side and instinctively diving in after it. Then getting ground into a barley blob.

I look at the empty wooden washbacks that hold the liquid once it's drained from the tun and imagine myself getting screamed at for dumping 150 kilos of yeast into the wrong one, as if the yeast bags will magically appear in my hands, open on their own and then pour over the side. Or, I feel myself falling twenty-five feet to my splatting doom at the bottom of the empty washback, or even worse drowning in the alcohol-and-carbon-dioxide pool of a full one. In each case, my paranoia is careful to ignore the fact that I'd have to climb four feet to reach the lip of the gigantic barrel, and I may just possess the physical prowess to avoid accidentally climbing over the edge.

I've been on the job for three minutes and all I can think about is how I will screw this up and have the frustrated natives toss me into the sea that brought me to their sanctuary.

ELEVEN

AYE, AYE, AYE

"Should I pretend that I have a limp?" I ponder as I examine my new coworker hobble across a catwalk.

Having so far survived my first day in the mash house, my mind turns to what I can do to enhance my standing as a new member of the distillery crew. I've been introduced to the skill of mashing by Thomas, a former fisherman-turned-whisky guy. I've quickly learned that much of the mashing process consists of standing around waiting for water to fill the gigantic tub, watching it soak barley and then waiting for water to drain. I picture the skulls of American corporate officers, efficiency consultants and management technique authors exploding into thousands of tiny shards at the thought of a worker standing around with no "busy work" to make them appear vital. Yet, that's exactly the case with Thomas.

Once in a while he needs to go to the mill house to make sure grain is being ground into grist for the mashing process, or he has to move bags of yeasts to the washback room in preparation for fermentation. But, for the most part, he quietly stands around and watches water.

Thomas is probably in his early forties. It's hard to tell here on the island, where men's bodies are an extension of the environment around them. They wear the windblown landscape in the lines around their eyes, the salty sea air in the cracked skin on their hands, and the rocky hills in their every step. Thomas is shorter than me by at least eight inches, and his hair has seen days of darker color and denser follicles. He moves between pipes, valves, and up and down the staircase with intelligent confidence when the sporadic calls for action come.

I've tried conversing with him and have drawn out the sparsest of information about a fishing background, but for the most part our conversation has this level of intensity:

"Distillery life must a bit more secure than fishing."

"Aye."

"Did you ever run into dangerous situations while fishing?"

"Aye."

"I heard distillery life can be dangerous, too. A guy in the warehouse had to have his finger reattached?"

"Aye."

"Is there anything else you'd like to do, career-wise?"

"Aye."

"This job gives you plenty of chances to stare at the barley and malt and be alone with your thoughts without being bothered by people or having to talk to them at all, doesn't it?"

"Aye."

Without the benefit of conversation to distract me, my thoughts turn to other things, such as Thomas's limp. I noticed it right away when I met him, though it's subtle. Subtler than the guy in the still house. And his is subtler than the guy in the bottling hall. I'm beginning to think that the limp is a stamp of authenticity here.

The quasi-carpal tunnel syndrome I developed from years spent in front of computers at my office jobs wouldn't impress in this work environment. Maybe I can stick a matchbook inside a boot, beneath my heel, to get my own little limp. It's an old trick I learned about altering your appearance from reading the *Hardy Boys*. Trust me; I can change my entire identity in a heartbeat thanks to that clever duo.

I really want a good limp with a good backstory. Like a pallet plummeting into my hip...a conveyer belt snapping off and cracking my shin...or shattering my ankle while stopping a runaway forklift before it crashed into an old-timer on his retirement day – I like that one. A limp and a story would give me instant blue-collar cachet to make up for my resume of working-class disasters. I wouldn't be so thoroughly insecure and self-conscious with my every word and move if I adopted a fake limp. Thomas and his colleagues would eagerly embrace me into the brotherhood of manual labor without question if I wobbled a bit with every step.

Adaptation is my emergency escape from myself, my secret disguise so I can try to fit into any situation without being noticed as not fitting. One of the benefits of growing up with little sense of self is that you can mask that by becoming whatever you need to be to function at any given moment. And when all your heroes are fictional, well, it sparks the imagination into more complex, fanciful masquerades.

Males my generation and younger don't have guides to tell us how to confidently be men. All we have is *Playboy*, beer commercials, sitcoms where the adult "guys" act like they're fourteen years old, and SportsCenter highlights of married millionaire athletes who get caught running around like sixteen-year-olds who just discovered what their penises can do. Somehow, out of our male entertainment resources, we're supposed to learn how to stand tall in the world, be captains of capitalism and freedom fighters, and still serve as pillars for the women in our lives who are themselves being pulled in five hundred directions. We're expected to be ourselves when everything we see and hear is telling us how to be anything but strong individuals. The contrast is intensely confusing and confounding, which makes adaptation all the more appealing.

Subtly adjusting to a situation numbs my sharp stab of insecurity. My voice becomes softer, higher, and my vocal rhythms more feminine when I feel trapped among more dominant people: namely men who are in power positions. I'm vocally deeper, more abrupt and dismissive when I need to seem like an in-charge expert. From those two bases spring forth an entire cast of Rob characters, which is why I've been described as everything from priest-like to absolutely evil and have played every role possible between the two extremes.

I'm going to resist the urge to limp. I've limped my way through too much of my life with artificial emotional appendages. If I can't walk proudly and confidently into this unknown world in which I have now entered, then I might as well go home and curl up into a limp ball. And, after that day in the twenty-third-floor office, I've no desire to find myself floor-bound in the fetal position again. So, I'll try something new for a change: authenticity.

TWELVE

SQUARE IN CIRCLE

The longer I spend here in the mash house, the more I understand Thomas's lack of interest in conversation. This is a living world of proud pipes, moody machines and bubbling, boiling barley. He doesn't have to talk to anyone because he's so involved listening to all the intrigue that's around him.

Most of the action revolves around mechanical siblings. The grist hopper, I'll call her Griselda, is the aloof eldest. She's not very attractive – browned-butter in color, boxy and clunky, with an elephant snout of a nose. But, out of that nose pours the grain that drives this whole train.

The mash tun, Tubby, her slightly younger, plodding brother, is a twenty-five-foot-wide basin that accepts Griselda's grain mixed with boiling hot water without complaint. He tries to mask his brutish size with a delicate blue coat of paint and gold trim, but when his five-armed, toothy snarl of a mouth starts grinding through the grain, it's sadly clear that people will only see him as a tool.

Standing separate from the eldest siblings are the hyperactive twins: two brew tanks that vie for constant attention. Mary Kate and Ashley are always pushing and pulling at Tubby, either filling him with hot water, or draining him and taking the liquid sugars pulled from the grain. Poor Tubby does the bulk of the work, but the twins get to rush the sweetened wort to the fermentation room three times a day, earning wide praise for their effort.

This little family is held together by their multitasking Mama who organizes a dizzying system of copper pipes that ferries the liquid from stage to stage. And the proud Papa pagoda that houses all these drink-producing devices stands majestically above his family, keeping everyone warm and safe.

Thomas is a kind of Mary Poppins without an umbrella, not even to help steady that limp. Thomas makes sure the family gets along. If Griselda refuses to give up all her grain, or if Tubby gets stuck, or the twins decide not to cooperate, he is there to coax, cajole and crack them along the side of the head with a pipe wrench if necessary.

In my lifetime, scientists have unlocked much of the mystery of life through DNA extraction and analysis. They've mapped so many genes they can practically predict whether or not you're predisposed to crying at a wedding (I am). Long before gene splitters, computer sequencing and stem cells, the monks who invented whisky had the basics of genetics figured out. They knew based on the grains they used what the end flavor would be.

Though I know about these basic principles and the chemistry concepts behind whisky flavors, I am still in awe. Today's mash is of a different barley variety than yesterday's, and the olfactory distinction between them is immediately evident. The mash house must be about a hundred degrees, and Thomas and I are in our sixth hour of silence. My ears ring from the constant clang of machinery and every pore on my body has sucked in and retained the grainy odor steaming through the air. Through it all I can pick out a faint fruity aroma that will remain with and enhance the final whisky product – much different from yesterday's smokier barley.

In fact, more than the grain is infused in the whisky at this stage. Water gathered from the distillery's local source, in this case a stream that runs alongside Bruichladdich, also adds its influence. Bruichladdich's water doesn't have the same intense peat or vegetative aspects that mark the water at several other Islay distilleries. It's crisp and ripe, with earthy minerals that give heft to the barley's fruitiness.

No matter what you do along the whisky-making process, you will never eliminate the "DNA" delivered at this stage of development. No amount of cask "therapy" will ever erase those imprints from youth. These characteristics will be present from beginning to end. The circle of whisky life.

Twice in my life, circles made imprints that I carry with me, even if others can't see them.

*

Preschool. It's the first day of my life that I am without a family member in my presence to protect me. There is no grandparent, aunt, uncle or distant cousin to babysit me; I'm left to strangers. At least I have my best friend, Joey, who lives three houses down from me. His mother convinces mine to enroll me at this church-run preschool. I shake as Mom walks me through the colorless and ominous neoclassical church doorway and into the community room.

There must be thirty kids in the room, a cavernous recreation hall that makes me feel even smaller than I am. Mom leaves after pinning a "Robby" nametag to my shirt and introducing me to the head teacher, Jean. I meekly follow Jean while searching to see if Joey is looking for me so we can play together. Every time I spot him among the weaving swarm of graham-cracker-clutching kids, he is engrossed with playing...playing with someone who is not me. I've never seen him have other friends and am dazed as I walk through this world outside our neighborhood. Jean leaves me alone in a play area that has kid-size costumes among the toys. I don a Robin Hood hat because its coolness is something I can hide behind. I play Sherwood Forest alone in a corner, out of sight of the other kids and my non-friend friend, Joey.

Jean and her helpers call out and wrangle the children with such systematic authority that I am paralyzed as to what to do. The kids start to sit. Every instinct inside me screams to hide behind the rest of the kids, but there is no backside. They are forming a gigantic circle, and I'm sure to be spotted by half the room if I hide. I furtively look for Joey, but he is hemmed in by other kids, and pays me no attention. My only spot to sit is on the other side of the circle from him. I quietly slide to the floor and hide under the Robin Hood hat as best I can.

"Good morning, everyone!" Jean says slowly and smilingly, as she casually rolls a large rubber ball on the floor in front of her splayed legs.

"Good morning, Jean!" the kids shout back gleefully. My heart races as I dread that the others noticed I didn't respond.

"We are going to play 'the name game' this morning!" she enticingly reveals, eliciting chatter, claps and an impromptu dance by one small boy who is gently reminded to return his rear to the floor.

"Everyone spread your legs apart so you can catch the ball."

A flurry of movement later and all the kids have their legs spread widely, me included. This isn't so bad, now that I'm adapting to the moment. No one caught me failing to say Jean's name. No one seems to be judging the angle or width of my leg-spread. I can quietly and comfortably sit here unnoticed.

"Let's start!" Jean says, and most of the kids sit up straight in eager anticipation of...I don't know. Jean hasn't exactly explained "the name game."

"Jean rolls the ball to...Robby!"

I become a statue, aside from my eyes, which frantically scan the circle for another Robby. Jean is half a mile away and the ball she just rolled is getting closer and closer. I venture a partial head movement to my right. Two girls are immediately next to me. Highly doubtful they are Robby. I glance back to see that the ball has now reached the center of the circle and is still heading in my direction. Looking left, I see a boy next to me who could be a Robby...except his nametag says David. Nametag!!! I look down. Somewhere in all the excitement, I'd forgotten about the nametag that was pinned to my shirt.

I quickly scrutinize the nearby nametags, taking full advantage of the advanced reading skills my patient mother has taught me. I see no "Robbys."

"Get ready, Robby!" Jean shouts.

I whip my eyes back and there is no mistaking the gravity of the situation. The ball is making a beeline for my Granimals. In slow motion, I reach out to the ball and halt it, inches from my groin. The room comes to a standstill. All eyes are upon me. My breath wheezes to a stop. Maybe they won't notice me. Except, I have the damn ball between my legs. This is a pickle.

"Now it's your turn, Robby!" Jean says. "Do what I did and call out someone else's name when you roll it to them."

Do what I did... That is a direction I can fulfill. I've learned that if I don't follow orders, it doesn't bode well for my backside. And I'm not about to let that happen. Besides, this is finally the chance to get back on Joey's radar. *Do what I did...*

"Jean rolls the ball to Joey!" I say with loud confidence as the ball flies from my fingers. The ball has barely cleared my knees when I hear the first laugh. By the time it passes my feet, the entire room has erupted in laughter. I whirl my head to Jean, who has giggled herself into a deep shade of red.

"You're supposed to say *your* name, not *my* name!" she bellows at me, and a second wave of shouts and snickers pounds me.

Panicked, I look for support from Joey. The ball has nearly reached him. His right hand is outstretched. But it isn't in position to stop the ball. His index finger pierces my Robin Hood persona like a crossbow bolt. I can't hear him through the cacophonous cackles, but I read his lips: "You're Jean! You're Jean!"

There's nowhere to hide in a circle...

This circle is nearly six hundred people in diameter. We aren't sitting with our legs splayed. Some people are cross-legged, others are lounging on their elbows in the grass and a couple of significantly unwashed dudes are playing hacky sack. We are the incoming freshman class at Colorado College. It is orientation week and this gigantic circle on the quad in front of one of the dorms is the foundation for an icebreaker.

Most college orientation weeks consist of paperwork and parties. Colorado College is an innovative and experimental liberal arts institution. Our orientation-week fun started with discussion groups analyzing a book about involuntary manslaughter we were required to read over the summer; moved on to a day of small group icebreakers where we revealed our names and opinions on labor laws; and has culminated here, on the quad.

I've been living in Colorado for the past three months, having dramatically departed Wisconsin after the heartbreaking conclusion of my only glimpse of a relationship, the high school dream queen Sabrina. Every day that I walked into the doors of the McDonald's where I worked in the small town of Castle Rock, I took a further step away from the confidence I surrounded myself with my last two years of high school popularity. With every Happy Meal I packaged for squealing tykes, I wrapped myself deeper into my unhappy childhood.

By the time I've reached this freshman orientation circle, I am a right mess: part high school leader; part fast-food fool; part worthless working-class kid; part four-year-old Jean. I've outgrown the need to completely hide, which is good, as I learned on that fateful day fourteen years ago that you can't hide in a circle. But, who am I in this circle? There is no name-tag to give me identity.

I feel I am nothing like the rest of these kids who've come from some of the most elite prep schools in America to one of the top twenty colleges in the country. A few have cars that are worth more than my parents' home. Even the second-generation hippies are wearing what could be best described as designer rags. The guys my age all seem older than me. They are strapping and self-assured in comparison to my emaciated pimply body. They seem traveled, worldly, confident and far smarter than the repetitive voice in my head that keeps sneering, "Rob is stupid."

The large icebreaker is led by upperclassmen, the resident assistants who will be our guides and monitors throughout our first year of campus life. They trod the sunny quad trying to garner the attention of six hundred people. Collectively, they don't possess the attention-grabbing authority of my old pre-school teacher, Jean. Then again, we eighteen-year-olds don't possess the ability to follow instructions that a group of pre-schoolers has. After what seems like an entire afternoon, silence is finally obtained and one of the leaders explains the next team-building icebreaker.

"We have such great diversity here..." he starts out. I look around at 592 white kids and eight darker ones as he continues his pep talk.

"Each of us brings a different perspective and comes from a unique place..." Apparently, my unique place doesn't include the Birkenstock store that shod the majority of feet here.

"...but collectively we have a voice that can speak to the world. Our next exercise will be to find that voice. We are going to create a class chant!"

Excited whoops and hollers bounce off the surrounding dorms and class buildings. Unfortunately, they all come from the other resident assistants. The new freshman class looks at each other with a visual, "get me the hell out of here." However, we collectively capitulate if for no other reason than to quell the peppy prodding of the resident assistants.

One of the more boisterous girls I've seen this week shouts out.

"Open the vodka, pour the beer, we're gonna rock ya, our class is finally here!"

Hundreds of cheers erupt and the resident assistants break out in laughter. I even make a wry comment to someone sitting next to me. Someone I've never met. I spoke to them first. Wow. Maybe this college thing won't be so bad. I feel the high school leader stepping in front of my other personas.

Now that the ice is broken, the penultimate goal of the icebreaker, other people chime in with ideas. There are many more drinking jokes, a couple of drug chants, a few esoteric references and some attempts at idealistic profundity (albeit more in the vein of Bob Marley than Immanuel Kant), but no one has found a way to bring these elements together into a cohesive whole. The resident leader recognizes this.

"These are some fantastic ideas. What we need to do is find a way to structure them into a chant that is representative of all of them. How can we do this?" he asks, sending six hundred people back into collective silence.

He's right. A structure of some sort is needed. Even using the melody from the chorus of a well-known song and connecting these thoughts as catchy lyrics would work...

"How about 'I Am the Walrus'?" I hear a voice say as the words vibrate along my vocal cords. Oh. My. God. I didn't...

A year earlier, for my high school senior homecoming, we had to develop a class chant as part of the homecoming contests. My brilliant idea was to use the chorus of "I Am the Walrus" as a base for the chant, replacing it with "We Are the Saders" (our mascot was a Crusader). I wrote lyrics that encapsulated our class spirit built around the "We Are the Saders" theme. It wasn't very good. In fact, it was so bad that my classmates wisely and rightly rejected it. I am dumbfounded that the idea has reared its awful head again. Only this time, I don't know these classmates. And instead of sixty, there are six hundred. How did my mouth open and words come out? *Why did my mouth open and words come out?*

Six hundred faces stare at me with a silence that is louder than the laughter of my preschool peers all those years ago. I no longer feel I am nothing like them. They are nothing like me. A scared four-year-old who has ventured too far out of his neighborhood. The square in this round gathering.

*

I stare into the mash tun and watch the water slowly drain from the steaming mush of grain. For better or worse, the elements the water takes away from the barley in this giant iron circle are going to stay with the whisky for its entire existence. Thomas is standing next to me, also gazing at the grain, away in his own world. I wonder how old he is right now.

THIRTEEN

THE HIGHS AND LOWS OF ISLAY

Nightmares often woke me in the early morning hours during my first few weeks on Islay while living at the farm cottage. I would blink my eyes open to find absolute darkness and hear nothing but screaming wind from the frequent winter gales that thrashed the island. My first instinct would be to reach for the comforting arms of Katie as I struggled to understand the fast-fading images from my subconscious. As lucidity took hold, I would understand that she wasn't there. No one was there. I was alone. And I knew within that absence lay the source of my nightmares. I would eventually drift off to sleep again, sometimes to repeat the same confused break from slumber, but always wake up to great relief when daylight would finally arrive and the nightmares would be gone for at least another half day.

As much as the isolation haunted me at night, I welcomed it during the daylight hours when the rain would stop long enough for me to get outside and explore the surrounding land. I embraced the return to the outdoor wanderings of my childhood and found time to contemplate the major life changes of the past two years.

Directly beyond my cottage's back gate stand several hundred acres of pastureland, bogs, thin streams, rising hills and scattered ruins. One of the advantages to living on an island is there is a limit to how lost you can find yourself. Fearlessly, I often set out with no plan, no direction to head, only a desire to stay as dry as possible. Even with Gortex boots and the finest Columbia raingear, water dangers abounded.

In winter, Islay is green and brown, but there are subtle variations within those color palettes. Through trial and error, I learned by the color of vegetation which flora had relatively solid, if squishy, ground beneath it. The error part was finding out that I was wrong by plunging up to my shins, and occasionally knees, into a bog.

My favorite spot is atop Cnoc Abhail, a hill that rises nearly three hundred feet near the cottage. When I climb it, I sit with my back against a four-foot-tall land boundary marker, the side I lean against determined by which way the wind bellows – usually at thirty miles per hour or more.

A year ago I was in an office in downtown Los Angeles and a year before that having discussions with Katie about what we would name our children. Now, I'm by myself, atop a hill on a remote island. The few roads I can see from here occasionally have cars on them. Within eyesight are a few small groupings of homes. When I think about the people behind the wheel or inside the houses, I wonder what their lives are like. Are they working jobs that are eating away at their spirits? What heartbreaks wake them in the middle of the night? If they could run off to find the life answers that elude them, where would they go? On top of the hill, I feel connected to people who don't even know I'm here. Up here, I don't feel as alone as I do when I'm inside the cottage in the middle of the night. This spot makes me feel at home.

Distilling Rob: Manly Lies and Whisky Truths

To the west stand the dark, fir-covered hills framing Loch Finlaggan. With a good squint, I can even make out the remains of the Finlaggan stronghold, where the rulers of the west coast of Scotland held court six hundred years earlier. Those ruins are babies compared to the Neolithic standing stone in front of them that has watched over the loch since being erected a thousand years before the birth of Christ. Both sights humble me to the point where I can occasionally let go of my ego and realize my problems are going to be lost to time, like everything else eventually is.

To the south, I see little shades of children running around the schoolyard at Keills, a hamlet of a dozen homes and apartments next to my bus stop. Grazing cows and sheep spread out in the fields outside the village, but they tend to stay clear of the ugly communications tower that rises inappropriately close to a small, seven-hundred-year-old cemetery. Most of the tombstones there are weathered beyond recognition, if they're standing at all. I suppose the dead's dislike of the tower can't compete with the living's love of mobile phone access. It may be ugly, but without it, my smartphone is useless.

I much prefer looking to the mysterious, enticing north. The first thing that arrests my vision are the Paps of Jura on Islay's neighboring island. For much of the winter, they've been dusted with, and sometimes caked under, snow. The contrast of the white-coated purple mountains to the icy blue Sound of Islay is bold, but can't compare to the breathless view of the Paps against the North Sea that stretches into oblivion beyond the lighthouses at the tips of Jura and Islay. I can only imagine the heart-stop someone would have had looking out to the end of the world from my vantage point to see the tall masts of Viking warships sailing in their direction. Involuntary micturition comes to mind.

My favorite view is looking east. From here, I can see the forests of Dunlossit that stretch from the sheep pastures down to Islay's shores, the entire flow of the Sound of Islay, the awesome scope of Jura, and on a clear day the dark shape of the Scottish mainland. It's from here I can also see the ferry come in, my ferry, bringing new sets of eyes to see spectacular Islay.

For a month, I watched ferry arrivals and imagined what it would be like to have regular interaction with people again. Now that I am living here at the distillery, I'm able to leave that life of solitary wonder in the hills behind the cottage.

Bruichladdich's nineteenth century guesthouse is an interesting combination of bed and breakfast, hostel and corporate housing. The guesthouse is within eyeshot of two massive whisky warehouses, earshot of the nearly perpetual humming of the still house, and within noseshot of the mash house and its grainy aromas. Two cozy lounges are separated by an informal dining room. The bedrooms are on the upper level, the first floor as it's called in the UK, with names like the Taxman's Room, the Cooper's Room, and such, to maintain the whisky theme.

When you've been in virtual isolation, as I've been for the past month, there is a kind of giddy excitement that arises upon the prospect of meeting people, much like my time in Hollywood when I knew I'd see a celebrity at an event. In this case, Euan, an electrician from Glasgow spending a few weeks rewiring Bruichladdich, is my Ewan McGregor; Bruce, the IT contractor here for a few days to upgrade the distillery's computers, is my Bruce Springsteen; Mary the cook is my Madonna; and the perpetually pink-clad house manager Margaret is my, well, Pink.

I revel in Euan's muddled Glaswegian accent and have a hearty conversation based on the half of his words I understand. I flirt away with grandmotherly Mary and Margaret every morning after my ten-thousand-calorie Scottish breakfast. The joy I have of being with people again has also helped me sleep. The nightmares I had at the cottage disappeared the first night I stayed here and haven't returned since.

In addition to conversation, the distillery has given me transportation. Duncan has generously allowed me to use the distillery's Volkswagen van during off hours whenever I feel like it. I'm only fifteen miles from the cottage, but between talking to new people and having wheels of my own, I might as well be a world away from where I've been the past month.

*

Two months have passed since I was last behind the wheel of a vehicle. My plan this evening is to drive two miles to the small coastal village of Port Charlotte to have dinner at a local restaurant. My first dinner out since arriving on Islay. A chance for some local nightlife. As I open the driver's door, my lack of recent driving time doesn't cross my mind. I'm too excited about immersing myself in local culture without having to worry about catching a bus to take me back to the cottage before sunset. I sit down inside the van, close the door, locate the seatbelt and stretch it across my body. Click. I'm ready to go. I raise the keys to the ignition.

There is no steering wheel.

Perplexed as can be, I try to grasp how a vehicle can't have a steering wheel. I immediately look around the vehicle to see what else is out of place.

The steering wheel is on the passenger side.

"Oh, shit," I blurt as I grasp the situation.

Everything is on the other side here, isn't it? My heart hammers as I think about that tow-truck mirror I ripped off the first, and only, day I drove one. Anxiously, I exit the van to move to the other side. My feet slip a little bit on the icy pavement. Double shit. It's icy. It's icy and I am going to have to drive on the wrong side of the car after not driving for two months. Can this get any worse?

Yes.

The ignition is easily found when I reach the right/wrong driver's side of the van. However, the gearshift isn't on the steering column. And there's an extra pedal next to the brake and gas pedals: the clutch for a stick shift, which I haven't driven in years. On the wrong side. And then I notice the shift box is on the dashboard, not the floor. At this point, I ponder whether it is even worth it to drive in this bizzaro universe of opposites. What the hell is up with the British, anyway? First they give us this system of measurements that makes no sense, which they abandon without telling us Americans. Then they go and put all their cars on the left side of the road, which goes against the natural right-handedness most of us possess. No wonder they lost an empire. They probably put that in the wrong place, too.

I hold an internal debate about whether or not to go on this excursion. At this point, I'm in a near panic thinking about how many times I've screwed up "adult" things the first time I tried them. Maybe I'll give up, go back to the guesthouse and have dried pasta and canned sauce for dinner.

No. I haven't come to this island to live in apprehension. I refuse to give in to the same trepidation that has clutched me much of my life. I firm my jaw, steady my gaze, start the van, shift into reserve, and confidently let the clutch fly and the gas flow…

…My flashlight slowly illuminates where the bumper has banged the barrier that stood forty feet behind me just a few seconds earlier. Some scrapes, and yes, perhaps a dent. I look around the distillery courtyard. No one has heard or seen anything. I nod resolutely. I don't care if I end this night with just a steering wheel in my hand; I am not going to run away from this challenge.

"There is no give-up in Gard," I reaffirm to myself as I take a purposeful stride back to the beast that bucked me.

My feet fly out from under me and my ass lands with a loud crunch on the ice.

FOURTEEN

THE WIZARD OF LOCHINDAAL

White knuckles are a clear sign of gripping something too tightly. After getting behind the wheel of the wrong-sided van and creeping along icy coastal roads, my knuckles are alabaster. Thankfully, they are no longer wrapped around a steering wheel, but around a glass of Scotch. I am at a pub inside the Lochindaal Hotel in Port Charlotte following an eternal two-mile drive. God decided he had enjoyed enough laughs for the night and I'd arrived without incident, save for the seven-minute attempt at parallel parking in this opposite-side universe.

Port Charlotte can be driven through in under a minute. Ninety percent of its whitewashed nineteenth century buildings line the main coastal road with a few more scattered along the village's two side streets. The village is a port in name only, as the sole pier that protrudes from the waterfront is unused by residents and too neglected to be an attractive backdrop for tourists. I think it's about 7:30 p.m., though it's so hard to tell when the sun sets shortly before 4:00 p.m. I do know it's early enough that I would expect to see some signs of life out and about, but my marathon parallel-parking endeavor was unimpeded by traffic and unobserved by passersby.

My attempt for a night out at a lively pub has resulted in me sitting alone in the Lochindaal, aside from a bartender/handyman who keeps the small dining-area fireplace heated by burning empty plastic bottles, used napkins and other trash. The hotel is named after the adjacent sea loch and feels like it was last decorated and cleaned in 1973. If there's a dust mite in here younger than me, I'd be surprised.

Finishing my Scotch, I ask to see a dinner menu. The bartender, Roger, looks back at me with a "that's an interesting request" expression.

"I'll have to check with the chef to see if he has any food," Roger responds after waiting to see if I'm going to deliver a punch line to render my request a joke. I size up his response, waiting for a punch line of his own. We realize each of us is viewing this situation as being strange, though for different reasons. I'd have to give his reality the edge. Outsiders don't come to this place, this time of night, this time of year. From the looks of it, locals don't either.

Left alone for ten minutes, I consider reaching behind the bar and walking off with a few bottles of rare Scotch that are entombed beneath cobwebs, but I doubt my ability to propel the getaway van to an escape before dawn rolls around. Finally, a door opens and out walks a gray-haired, wiry man in his late fifties wearing a chef's jacket and pajama bottoms.

"Whatcha doing here?" he inquires in a Scottish rat-a-tat that is driven by curiosity rather than annoyance.

"Well, I was hoping to get dinner."

"No, whatcha doing *here*? No one's around here now. I'm glad you came in. I'll take care of you. We don't have much, but I'll cook you up something good. We're busier in the summer, and I have all kinds of food, but not much now, not much now. But, I'll take care of you. Name's Matthew, by the way," he points to the name on his chef's jacket. "But, you can call me Matty."

Matty has the energy and attention span of a five-year-old that has swallowed four tubes of Pixy Stix and washed them down with a Red Bull. He veers off on tales of being a chef in Glasgow and the Caribbean before coming to Islay two years ago for...he's vague about the reason. I pull him back from a story about Swedish skinny-dippers in front of the hotel last year in an attempt to move him forward on my food.

"Ah, right, right. Don't worry, I'll take care of you. What do you want tonight?"

"Do you have fish?"

"Yes."

"I'll just have some fish and vegetables, please."

"No, no, no," Matty negates, leaving me wordless. "I don't feel like making fish tonight." I'm at another impasse, waiting for a punch line that won't come.

"Well, what can I have?" I finally ask.

"Don't worry, I'll make you up something good."

"I don't eat beef or pork, only chicken and fish."

Matty doesn't respond. He seems lost in his own world of recipes. He snaps back to the present and slaps me on the back.

"I'll take care of you!"

Matty appears fifteen minutes later. He brings me a freshly prepared soup, a garden's worth of steamed vegetables and a succulent-looking chicken breast stuffed with...

"Matty, what is this chicken stuffed with?"

"Haggis."

"I don't eat red meat at all, remember?"

"It's not red meat. It's haggis!"

With that he slaps me on the back again and disappears behind the door where he first appeared. Once again, I'm left alone in the bar, this time feeling exhausted. No surprise there are no Port Charlotte residents out and about – Matty has stolen all their energy. I take a bite of the chicken crammed with sheep's stomach stuffed with meat.

"Damn, that's good," I say to the empty room, as I feed my hunger in the atmospheric glow of melting plastic bottles.

*

Eating alone was normal for me for a number of years. There's a great *Magnum P.I.* episode where he plays a dangerous game of love and theft with a striking English beauty. In the end, he wins, and loses, by outmaneuvering her in a showdown between crime and protection. Our mustachioed hero waits hours for her arrival at the finest restaurant in Hawaii, knowing with each passing moment his call to duty means she had no choice but to bid him an escaping goodbye. The coolest man in the Pacific Rim ends up eating dinner alone, drinking his own condolence. Strong, melancholy, mysterious. I always tried to imagine myself looking like that when I ate out alone and had people sneak glances at me, speculating what great adventure had led me to be solo at their fine restaurant.

They probably thought I was just creepy.

In my first couple of years at college, I often ate alone in the dining hall, especially if there were no easy openings at a table with the few friends I'd made. I would then brood à la Magnum, trying to look like I was recovering from an intriguing mystery. Even if seven of my friends were around a table of eight chairs, I'd sit alone at a back table rather than draw attention to myself by trying to join them. What if they didn't want me there? What if they were talking about me? I was such an invisible figure to myself that I'd have people stand twenty feet in front of me crossing the quad waving, and I wouldn't wave back for fear they were waving at someone behind me (which always seemed to happen on those few occasions I did wave back).

Ralph became a friend over two months of directing me in a play (despite terminal shyness, I always seemed to find a way to do something that brought attention to me). A few weeks after the play, he was one of those waving folks on the quad that I pretended not to notice. He verbally stopped me and asked if I remembered who he was. He wasn't kidding. My invisible self was so strong it was now making others feel invisible.

I felt horrible after my interaction with Ralph, for both him and for me. I was twenty years old, capable of drawing admiration from my professors for my intellectual acuity, able to walk out on a stage and inhabit a complex character, and incapable of stepping over my own emotional clumsiness. I made a vow that things needed to change. Immediately.

Several days later, I found myself with a breakfast tray in hand, looking for a place to sit in the dining hall. In the middle of the room, alone at a two-person table, is a girl my friend Ken knows. She is adoringly cute and based on what Ken says, extremely cool. I am now two years into brooding over Sabrina and being invisible is no way to meet a girl. I determine that this is the moment for my new, non-invisible self to debut. I don't actually remember how I make it from the food service area to her table. I presume I didn't run into anyone or drop anything, though I very well may have blocked that out; because, as soon as I reach the table, I certainly block out the skill of speech.

"Hello," she offers curiously to this beanpole boy standing in front of her. All I can do is nod back.

"Can I sit?" I wheeze through the throat that is constricted by the pounding in my heart and the shaking in my knees. This is better than invisibility?

"Absolutely!" she replies kindly, and I tremble to a seated position, spilling my cereal onto the tray as I set it on the table. I catch a sly smile cross her lips that conveys bemused pity.

"So, what's your name?" she asks, breaking the awkwardness.

"Rob," I sputter, trying to look at her and barely succeeding.

"Nice to meet you, Rob..." she lingers, waiting for me to ask the next logical question. However, she senses it isn't coming and provides the unprompted answer. "My name is Denise."

"Denise. Ken is my friend."

I am preceding the anti-suave gang from *The Big Bang Theory* by a few years with this exchange.

"Ken? Ken the basketball player?"

"Ken the basketball player. He's my friend. Ken the basketball player." Great. Now I've turned into Rain Man.

"He's a nice guy."

"Nice guy. Ken the basketball player. Nice guy."

"So...tell me about yourself?"

Oh goddammit, she didn't, did she? She did. She just threw the whole damn conversation on me! I think she believes this will help matters, but the poor girl doesn't fully grasp what she has quivering in front of her.

"Um. I like fish," comes out instead of my intended tale of a fishing trip I'd taken in the mountains the previous weekend.

"Me too. Anything else?" She is starting to have fun with this now. Considering her best other option is to call security, I suppose fun is the only way to go. "Do you like, I don't know, birds?"

Distilling Rob: Manly Lies and Whisky Truths

"Uh, yes. And mammals, too." Finally something genuinely funny comes out of my mouth, even if I was being serious.

"Well, Rob...Rob, right? Well, Rob, speaking of mammals I have a vertebrate zoology class in about twenty minutes, and I need to review a chapter. It was nice meeting you and maybe I'll see you again with Ken the nice guy basketball player."

With a smile she is gone, and I am in my familiarly alone dining position. Instead of my typical *Magnum P.I.* fantasy that I am sitting alone due to some secret lost love, I sit alone on this morning because I can't even talk to another human being. There is nothing romantic, nothing mysterious about my empty table. Only sadness.

FIFTEEN

THE SPACE BETWEEN SILENCE AND SCREAMS

Thomas limps his way toward one of the six pine washbacks in the tun room, and I follow him carrying a twenty-five-kilogram bag of yeast over each shoulder. For all the loud, metallic activity in the mash house where geyser-hot water extracts alcohol-producing sugars from the grain, the tun room, where the next stage in the whisky process takes place, is positively sedate.

Tun is the Celtic word for wineskin. Washbacks are the evolutionary descendants of those ancient wineskins, though significantly larger and much more difficult to carry over a shoulder. Each washback is a huge vat, in the case of Bruichladdich made of Oregon pine with a capacity of thirty-five thousand liters. Six of these twenty-five-foot-deep tubs stand in the tun room, with only the top four feet or so rising above the elevated grate that comprises the floor. Half of them contain liquid that is in varying stages of quiet fermentation. Heavy lids keep people like me from accidently tripping and falling in after somehow being launched four feet into the air. Yes, that's still a fear of mine.

Walking into the low-ceilinged tun room requires attention for those of us over six feet tall, as the pipe that pumps liquid into the tanks hovers smack dab in the middle of the main walkway. I believe Thomas tolerates my presence in his usually solitary world, but I'm still afraid all respect will be rescinded if I knock myself out by walking into the pipe and then falling into the exploded remnants of the yeast bags that I would inevitably drop upon losing consciousness. I make it into the room without incident as Thomas hooks a hose to the pipe to fill the appropriate washback. Today, it's the middle washback and my job is to add the yeast to the tun about twenty minutes into the forty-five-minute filling session.

Seven times a week, these wooden vessels are alternately filled and emptied of wort – the sugar-rich liquid from the mash house. The two strains of yeast I carry will devour this sugar-rich nectar and then multiply and grow. Within hours of being added to the wort, the new mixture starts to swirl, natural chemical processes cause the heat to rise significantly and a fermenting froth forms. Two days later, the froth reaches some six feet thick and the little yeasties have given birth to a kind of fruity and grainy beer called "wash" that is almost 10 percent alcohol.

"Is the wash drinkable?" I ask Thomas.

"Aye."

"Have you ever tasted wash?"

"Aye."

"Is it good?"

"Aye."

He silently, of course, offers me a taste of a wash that has fermented nearly three days. Some people say more than half the character of the final whisky product comes from the time it spends fermenting here. A short fermentation can make the whisky spicier and nuttier. A longer one can squeeze out grassy and fruity flavors. The liquid Thomas offers me has a tickling fizziness about it and tastes like a combination wine cooler/mead/wheatgrass potion.

Thomas and I dump the last two bags of yeast into the washback. The final inoculation that will help this whisky child prepare for its growth into a mature adult. It strikes me that Thomas does this dumping with a sort of gentleness. In fact, everything he does, from grinding the grain to mashing, hosing the washbacks to filling them, is done with the compassion of a father caring for a vulnerable child. Even his "Ayes" are delivered with a soft-spoken placidity. He seems like a truly nice guy. But, at this moment, my heart is breaking for him as I think back to an encounter I had last night.

Now that I've mastered the art of driving in an opposite universe – well, stopped running into things – I've started to make my visits to Port Charlotte a nightly occurrence. I know that in a few weeks I'll return to the isolation of the cottage. I want to interact with as many people and imbibe as many pints as I can before then. Sometimes it's only me, Roger and Matty at the Lochindaal. Other times, a handful of locals also drop in, usually to watch a football match or play a little pool.

The Lochindaal bar is divided into two rooms: the six-seat "restaurant" side and the pool-table side. Each side has a full bar, and a wide doorway through the bar connects the two for employees. Patrons must walk outside to get from one room to the next. Matty will handle one side of the bar while Roger works the other side when things get really busy. Really busy being three people on the restaurant side and six people on the pool-table side. Last night, Matty was firmly in charge of his part of the kingdom when it came to dealing with one of the regulars.

"Pint of lager," demands a young man as he walks into the bar. He is a day under twenty-one if he is anywhere near it at all.

Matty turns around and gives him a sincere tilt of the head and frown that indicates, "I feel bad about the news I'm going to deliver to you, but it has to be done."

"You broke my toilet, Alex. No more pints for you in here ever again," Matty says with a resigned sigh.

"No, I didn't!" Alex shoots back.

"Sorry, Alex, but you one hundred percent did last weekend. And the weekend before that, you broke my window in the same bathroom."

"Fuck! What the fuck? I didn't break the toilet!"

"Sorry, Alex. I'm one hundred million percent sure it was you."

"Give me a fucking pint!"

"Sorry, not a drop. You're out."

By now the other half-dozen folks in the bar have turned their gazes from the TV and the pool table to the unfolding scene.

"Just give me a fucking drink!"

"Not a chance. Sorry, not a chance," Matty says sadly, and takes Alex's hand and shakes it. "You're a problem. No more. Not a chance."

"I didn't fucking do it," Alex says, now sounding like the little boy who knows he did do it and there's no way out of the consequences.

"Not a chance. No more. Never again."

"Give me a fucking chance. Please." Alex pleads.

"You've had your chances. Sorry," Matty nods to the door, and Alex shuffles defeatedly into the night.

Distilling Rob: Manly Lies and Whisky Truths

During the course of this exchange a teenage boy had scooted up to the barstool next to me. I failed to mention that the Lochindaal's most devoted customers are local teenagers who come in for pool, a can of the favorite Scottish soft drink, Irn Bru, and, occasionally, when no one is looking, a smoke and a sneak of a forgotten drink left on the bar counter. This redheaded lad must be about fourteen and is an excellent pool player, from what I'd seen.

The boy shifts restlessly in his seat, not because of the situation, but because he is purely restless. Agitated in a way. He tries to draw Matty's attention to get a Coke, but Matty is busy opening two Budweisers for himself. The boy grunts with frustration and shifts again.

"I guess the lesson here is don't screw with Matty," I say to the boy, trying to distract him from his growing annoyance.

"Aye," he abruptly responds.

"Do you think the kid really broke the window and toilet seat?"

"Aye."

"There sure seem to be a lot of teens who hang out here."

"Aye."

There is something disturbingly familiar about this conversation.

"Does your dad work at Bruichladdich Distillery?" I probe. This does the trick. The boy stops fidgeting and turns to me.

"Yeah. He does," comes a defiant and defensive response.

"Is his name Thomas?"

The boy looks down and then away to the back of the bar. Matty is still engaged with his Buds.

"Aye," he finally responds.

"I've been working there and spending time with him in the mash house and tun room. He's a pretty nice guy," I say genuinely.

"He's a fucking idiot, is what he is. He just a fucking idiot!" The boy springs up from his chair and pounds on the bar. "Matty! I want a fucking Coke!"

Matty turns around and shrugs. He pops open the lid of a Coke and slides it across the bar. The boy grabs it and hustles away to the pool table.

*

Thomas gathers the empty yeast bags and gingerly shuts the washback lid. How could this quiet man elicit such a vociferous response from his own flesh and blood when he is so nurturing in the birthing stages of this young future whisky? He seems like the kind of dad who would dote on his son, though laconically. Then again, why is his teenage son in a bar night after night after night? Just because Thomas is good with barley doesn't mean he's good with a boy. Or is his son doing what nearly every boy has done in his attempt to become a man and thoughtlessly pushed his father away?

You could let this wort sit in the washback for twenty hours or you could let it sit in here for two hundred hours. It would look the same. There is a window, however, between 40 and 110 hours, when it reaches optimal maturity. If you stop the process too soon, the yeast hasn't had the chance to help the wort mature properly and it tastes like bad bread. If you don't show it enough attention and let it go unchecked on its own, all the sweetness that comes from its barley birth turns bitter and harsh. Yes, no matter when you pull the wash out of the washbacks, the liquid looks the same; but, it's not.

Appearances aren't everything.

Distilling Rob: Manly Lies and Whisky Truths

There is no manual that exists that tells you how to be a father and raise a son. There's no test you can take to measure your level of communication with your children.

And there sure isn't a guide that tells you how to hear your father.

SIXTEEN

BLOODLINES AND BATTLEGROUNDS

My dad isn't supposed to exist.
My Aunt Sharon was the older sibling, born in 1943. She arrived during a blizzard that forced my grandma to be taken to the nearest hospital by sleigh from her farm. The pregnancy was so complicated that the doctor drove her sixty miles in his brand-new Buick in order for her to get a C-section at the nearest "city" hospital. Grandma developed septicemia and was thought to be on her deathbed. She survived, but the doctor told her that the damage done in the emergency procedure, plus the additional complications, meant she couldn't have any more children.

Four years later, Dad came along. Son of a farm-girl mother and an any-job-he-could-keep father. He was an unremarkable boy who led an unnoticed life, running a paper route in his familiar neighborhood and delivering the news of a world far, far away. Then one day, he found himself out in that world.

He went to fight in Vietnam.

My eighteen-year-old angst consisted of a broken heart and memory stains from numerous childhood embarrassments. Dad's eighteenth year consisted of leaving behind an alcoholic father who beat him, and going to a country where people who had never heard of Beloit, Wisconsin, were trying to kill him. A kid whose lack of effort nearly failed him out of high school, now in charge of tracking multimillion-dollar fighter jets. I got stressed at McDonald's when the chicken nuggets took too long to fry and customers became irritable. If one of the products he was tracking didn't appear when expected, it meant someone was probably dead, blown up in the skies above a miserable jungle. I'd leave work in my McDonald's uniform and hear insults from local kids riding their bikes. He came home from his tour of duty to screams of "baby killer!" and chunks of spit flying at him from the mouths of long-haired, unwashed kids his own age.

Children are myopic when it comes to thinking outside of their own universe. Maybe it's nature's way of easing us into a world that is largely beyond our control. Maybe it's God's way of teaching us to develop compassion as we age and slowly learn to see other people as individuals with their own struggles and dreams. I only wish I could have stepped out of that ego cocoon sooner than I did when it came to my dad. I'll never know if more softness from me in my youth could have reduced his hardness. Instead, I met steel with steel, even knowing I would be defeated time and time again.

I never looked at him as an abused kid who was nearly killed by rockets in some tropical terror. I couldn't hear in his silence the smack of belt buckles on his skin, smell in his breath the reek of stale alcohol that hit him during his father's shouts, notice in his vacant stare in front of the TV any sign of the life that troubled him. All I knew was a guy who barely listened to me when I spoke, rarely helped me when I was growing up without criticizing me, didn't discipline me without bruising me and couldn't say he loved me without looking away. I saw a failed father, not a dad with demons. And, I did all I could to provoke those failings into actions that made us both suffer.

As in high school, I found that as the years passed in college, I slowly gained a sense of self-confidence. I acted a bit in plays and student films. I was a resident assistant in the freshman hall, helping newcomers transition to college a little less embarrassingly than I did. I even, through error and trial (and more error), managed to find a girlfriend. In what was to be a lifelong pattern in my dating life, Cami had issues with male trust, self-image and self-confidence, but she liked me and that's all I noticed at the time.

Of course, to keep her liking me, I was willing to do whatever Cami asked. Her repeated comments about how she loved long hair on men grew on me, along with my wavy mane. As my hair lengthened, I felt a sort of naughtiness rise inside me. The one-thousand-mile distance from my home had given me some defiance over Dad the past few years. I once went three weeks without answering his phone calls when he said my decision to take a theater directing class would ruin my life. The more adult responsibilities I took on – rent, groceries, part-time jobs – the less I felt I was under his control. So, I grew my hair because Cami loved it, but also because I knew Dad would hate it.

*

During one long break my senior year, I catch a ride back to Wisconsin to surprise my family. It's been some ten months since they last saw me and the hair that Dad told me to get cut at the time hasn't seen a scissors since. In fact, it is long enough to pull back into a short ponytail.

I'm devilishly curious about the reaction I will get from the man who still gets a buzz cut for his Air Force Reserve duty.

The look in his eyes when he sees me wipes away all of my newfound cockiness.

Breath escapes my lips with a whimper as the wall resounds with the thud of my body. I try to get around Dad's outstretched arms, but fail and once again am tossed backwards. I am only an inch or two shorter than he, but my emaciated frame can't compete with his Midwestern stoutness. I cower and snivel in a manner I haven't done in years. I may as well be 4 feet 1 instead of 6 feet 1, because I feel so small and impotent.

He hasn't acted out this aggressively in years, ever since he became a Born Again Christian. In fact, he's been a good and devoted father more often than not, trying to make amends for how he treated me when I was a child by being fully engaged with my brothers' lives. But now, we're both being thrown back in time. All because of the rubber band holding my hair back in a small ponytail.

"Get that goddamn thing out of your hair or I will cut it out, you stupid bastard!" he yells, lunging for the back of my head.

I try to dash out of the way and stumble over the couch.

"Stop!" I cry, not in defiance but in a plea for mercy.

"I won't have my son be some goddamn hippie!" he snaps as froth flies in my face. He grabs hold of the short ponytail and jerks my head forward. The rubber band is entwined in my hair. It's too difficult for him to get it out. He shoves me away and I slam against the wall again.

"Why do you do this to me?" he shouts, with tears edging his eyes. The hatred in his face has given way to weariness, but not over the physical match. In fact, I'm not even sure if he's talking to me at this point.

"I don't want to do this to my own son. Why do you make me do this? Do you know what I've gone through for this family and this country? I've given everything. Everything! And I have nothing to show for it."

I want to scream how much I hate him, but am struck with a kind of guilt that comes with speaking ill of the dead. He collapses into a chair, the weight of more than just my hair on his mind and in his heart. I bite my tongue. He looks sad and defeated.

"I'm sorry," I utter, knowing part of me deliberately went down this hair-growth path to see if I would get this kind of reaction.

"I know I wasn't a very good father to you when you were little," he finally says, unable to look at me. "I can never make up for that. I try to be better with your brothers, but I can't go back and change things with you.

"You never knew what my dad was like. He treated me worse than you can imagine because you don't know him like that. You know him as the nice grandpa. All I ever wanted was to be a better father than him. I thought that would be enough," he sighs wearily. "I tried to do the best I could."

"I know you did. I know," I can't find words beyond those. I slink out of the room and leave him alone.

Shortly thereafter, I cut my hair. I told myself at the time it was because I looked appalling with long hair. In retrospect, maybe part of it was because for the first brief time, I was able to see my father not as a dad, but as a man. And, I saw how hard that was.

SEVENTEEN

THE WAIT FOR WHISKY WISDOM

Today is my last day working with Thomas. Duncan has made plans for me to move on to the next stage of the whisky-making process, per Jim's directive. What I really want to do is spend time with Jim, learning from the master, but he is away again. I missed him during his brief return to the island before he headed to Germany for another conference. So, the next stage it is.

In truth, I am more than ready to move beyond the mashing and fermenting steps of the whisky process. Duncan isn't testing me on what I've learned, and he hasn't asked me to demonstrate my newfound abilities. I think he trusts that I've mastered the skill of watching barley get mashed and have the natural ability to dump yeast into huge tubs. If only my old Frito-Lay coworkers could see me now.

Thomas doesn't seem broken up by my impending departure at the end of today's shift. He doesn't seem anything by it. Aye, he's just Thomas. But, he's also a lot more than the quiet guy I met the first day of work. I can't shake something he revealed a few days ago in one of the few non-monosyllabic utterances he's had.

We were both quietly watching the barley steep, staring at the bubbling brown-gold primordial ooze, when, unprompted, he said:

"I always hoped I would have left Islay."

I waited for additional information, but he said no more. He just continued staring at the same scene he's watched thousands of times. I wasn't sure he knew he'd spoken aloud, so I didn't push the matter.

My time here has seen me look at the historic machinery and the condensation-soaked walls of this building with a sense of otherworldly wonder. Now, I wonder how Thomas sees them. Does he view the maze of pipes as the bars of a cell from which he'll never escape? Does his son run off to the pub because he senses his father would rather be anywhere but Islay? Or am I imagining it all, projecting my own fears of living life under the weight of being trapped in something I don't want?

Last year, I was in a work world where guys cockily tossed around words like "outside the box" and "deliverables" as though they were being issued from the mouth of God himself. They'd puff their chests out as they described strategic partnership implementation. Keyboards were their knives, boardrooms their battlefields, and happy hours were their hunting grounds. Masculinity through metrics. I hated it, but unlike Thomas, I was able to get away. I'm still confused as hell, but I don't live under the weight of unapproached hope. His comment has percolated in me these last few days the way the wort simmers along to full fermentation, but I haven't known what to do with it. I practically obsess on his words as we walk through the paces of our last day: staring at the mash as it soaks up water, draining it, filling it, staring, draining.

Distilling Rob: Manly Lies and Whisky Truths

Sauntering to the tun room. Pouring the wort into the washbacks. Dumping yeast. Pouring. Dumping.

During a prolonged staring session in the last hour of our shift, I finally ask Thomas a question that has bubbled to my mind's surface.

"Why did you choose to stay on Islay and make whisky, Thomas?"

If there's one lesson I've learned about Thomas, it's to ask a question that can't be answered with an "Aye." Thomas doesn't respond immediately, but I know he heard me.

The longer the question lingers in the air the more I expect Thomas to give me an answer that will rival that of the Dalai Lama. His "Ayes" have simply been masking the eloquent soliloquy that will spring from his lips. The deeper his gaze penetrates the grain the more inspirational the answer is becoming. I'm certain it will be something about reconnecting with the earth, with how his forefathers took the untamed, wild land God provided, and they shaped it by their sweat and sacrifice into providing a drink that connects the soul with the divine. He is a man among the mash, making a drink that the business boys from my former life swallow to help them get through their boisterously directionless existence.

I take in a deep breath of the grainy aroma and repeat my question.

"Why *did* you choose whisky making, Thomas?"

Finally, he looks up and locks his eyes with mine.

"I had a family and fishing was too dangerous. I took the job because I needed to take care of them."

"What?" I say almost accusingly.

"Aye. I don't even drink the stuff."

I'm left stunned as he turns and whacks a whining pipe with his wrench.

EIGHTEEN

THE ANGELS' SHARE AND THE DEMONS TAKE

Religion and whisky are strange bedfellows. The drink was invented by monks, probably by accident, but soon became a staple of life. Safer than the oft-contaminated drinking water of the Middle Ages, it had medicinal properties and warmed the body on those cold winter nights. Indeed, the water of life.

In the centuries since its invention, many Christian denominations have used the denouncement of alcohol as a tenet of their beliefs. It's a product of the devil. Drinking leads to immorality and loose living. Alcohol drives you to a lazy existence contrary to the hard work God put you here for. I'm not typically one to quote the Bible, but Proverbs 31:6-7 ("Give beer to those who are perishing, wine to those who are in anguish; let them drink and forget their poverty and remember their misery no more") strikes me as a fairly resounding theological directive to the contrary.

From the monks onward, whisky makers have known that the water of life is heaven-sent. In fact, God regularly collects rent on his provision through the long-held concept of the Angels' Share. Through every stage of whisky making, especially during aging in the cask, a certain percentage of alcohol is lost through evaporation. It is said to go into the mouths of angels that watch over and protect this celestial creation.

There is a certain redemptive quality to the Angels' Share. The Angels don't care if a whisky is young or old, if the character is hellacious or heavenly, if they can only touch a few fumes from the tun room or if they take their annual 2-percent evaporation allotment from casks. They accept what men may reject. They find the goodness in that spirit.

*

I returned to Wisconsin following my graduation from Colorado College because I didn't know what else to do. Four years away from home and four years of studies had me standing on the college quad after our graduation ceremony, looking to the Rocky Mountain range, and asking myself, "Now what?" A week later, I was back in my hometown, hating myself for failing to break away and never return, as I vowed when I was seventeen.

I quickly fell into the career of a journalist, thanks to some of my mom's connections. Journalism came easy to me, and I was soon one of the youngest newspaper editors in Wisconsin, running a weekly paper in the farming community of Clinton, a dozen miles outside Beloit. This success only added to the underlying depression of being back in Wisconsin. I had always viewed journalists as writers who weren't good enough to write anything else. My rapid ascension up the newspaper ladder made me wonder if I was merely an exceptionally mediocre writer.

My life resume grew as I expanded beyond running the newspaper. I served as president of the Clinton Chamber of Commerce, directed plays at the local high school and even had time to become an award-winning writer and producer for

Distilling Rob: Manly Lies and Whisky Truths

a Midwestern travel TV show. My professional confidence grew inch by inch, but my personal confidence remained shrunken. I hadn't had a date since my college girlfriend and I broke up after graduation. The only unmarried girls in Clinton seemed to still be in high school. And the few times I would meet a girl around my age, the experience was an exercise in linguistic paralysis. For me, an exciting social weekend was driving to Madison to play Dungeons and Dragons with bachelor friends. Really.

One winter night, with a frigid blizzard unraveling over Beloit, I decide to cancel my long distance drive to Dungeons and Dragons and instead invite local friends to join me for drinks at a smoky sports bar. As if Wisconsin had anything but smoky sports bars. This is a big step for me, because I don't like going to bars. I feel like an emaciated, pimply teenager among the loud, sturdy guys from my hometown who have the women that ignore me hanging all over them. For all the arrogance I had in college about how much better I was than this city, I now feel even smaller than before I had moved away.

The bar is hazy and bulging with the Saturday night crowd. My ears sting with the cacophony of basketball and hockey game broadcasts, thumping hip-hop coming from the small dance floor, shouts at the bartenders for cheap beer refills and a screeching girl fight that ends as one gal smashes a beer bottle over the head of another.

I'm alone at our table, as my friends have both the hip-shaking ability and personal confidence to get out on the dance floor. I sip a whiskey sour, trying to maintain a Bogart world-weariness. It's far more interesting to look like you *want* to be sitting alone at a table instead of looking socially stranded. The police haul off the two cat fighters, and activity returns to normal with my friends and others bumping and grinding on the dance floor while non-dancers like me stare at the hockey game.

Out of the corner of my eye, I notice a woman sitting at a table, alone like me, slowly swirling a straw in her cocktail. Blonde hair frames her very pretty face, unlike the hair of the many non-pretty women in here, which marches above their skulls in hairspray heaven. Her clothes sensually cling to her, rather than riding high and tight over exposed folds of supple skin like most of the other outfits here. She looks so bored, in her pretty black dress, alone against the wall while her friends go out and dance. Looking like a funeral while the party goes on without her smile.

She glances at my stare – one of the disadvantages to thinking you're invisible is you tend to stare long and obsessively, thinking no one notices you – and offers a wan smile. I give a goofy grin and turn away to my drink. For the next twenty minutes, we exchange cautious glimpses while my mind expels chaotic thoughts:

"What should you do, Rob? Walk up to her? No, can't do that, she might think I like her. What's wrong with that, idiot? What if she hates me? Good point. Maybe I can buy her a drink? What if she hates me? Damn. Why would she even want a drink from me? Or even want to talk to me? Look at her. She's beautiful! I'm wearing purple flannel. Purple? Why the hell purple? It was on the clearance rack. Dumbass, it's on clearance because no one else wants to buy it! Oh, great, now I'm wearing rejected clothes and she knows I'm cheap. I could go home and change, put on a black shirt. Oooh, then I could walk back in and say, 'Now our clothes match. Let's see if we do,' and wink. Jesus Christ! Just kill yourself now!"

Helplessly, I come out from inside my head and turn to her. My heart plummets as I see another man standing at her table.

Distilling Rob: Manly Lies and Whisky Truths

Actually, he clutches her table to steady his drunken dervish sway. The fear of him being a more suitable suitor subsides as I recognize who it is: Chris, a guy in his late thirties who looks twenty years older, and is one of our recognized town drunks. Yes, I come from a town with designated drunks. The unwashed and unkempt Charles Manson look-alike could be a Pentecostal poster child for a return to Prohibition.

My beauty squirms herself further against the wall as Chris leans in for conversation, a kiss or to steady his balance. It's hard to tell which and very well could be all three. I am paralyzed about what to do. In seconds I could be at her defense, turning him away and finding a reason to talk to her. In a few short strides I could be such a hero that she overlooks my purpleness and marries me on the spot. As I revel in this possibility, Chris's long, greasy hair skirts over her glass, sticking to the rim enough to knock it over, the liquid shrapnel soaking that lovely black dress completely. She screams at him to get away loud enough to bring her girlfriends stampeding from the dance floor to her defense.

Chris staggers away and, at the not-so-polite direction of a bouncer, is shown to the back door. The girls are having an intense discussion as they work to towel off the wet dress. I catch a bit of what the beauty in black says.

"I told you I don't fit in here! I just want to go home. Why did you drag me here? I should have just stayed home alone and read," she almost cries. I ache to comfort her, to tell her I feel the same way, to pull her out of here and go for a late-night coffee and honest conversation. Instead, I watch invisibly as the girls put on their coats and leave. They pass by me, and my fellow misfit, my beautiful angel, gives me a look of heartbreaking disappointment that seems to say, "I'd hoped you would've been my hero and saved me from this wretched place. You failed me."

The door shuts behind them, and I feel my stomach slam. I'm so worthless! I'm insignificant as a human being, let alone being anywhere near the man a woman would want. I'm pathetic. No good. Hero? Ha! Bogart would have me shot for being such a loser. No, he wouldn't even waste a bullet on me. I'm just an...

"Idiot! Idiot! Idiot!" I say aloud through clenched teeth.

"Huh?"

My friend Laura has returned to the table and my other friends are on the way back from the dance floor.

"Nothing," I mumble. "Talking about the hockey game."

With that, I grab my coat and leave.

The snow comes down so heavily I can barely see my car in the middle of the small parking lot. I take off for the two-minute-drive home, consumed by thoughts of being incapable of achieving the most basic requirement of human existence: finding a companion. I'm twenty-four years old, half my friends are married and the other half in relationships. And I can't even talk to a girl. I think about the bottle of whiskey I have back at the apartment and about the bottle of codeine pills in my medicine cabinet. I've been pumping large amounts of both into my body on a nightly basis, ever since I attended the wedding of my high school love, Sabrina, a couple of months ago, sitting alone in a church pew watching her find happiness. Maybe tonight I should go for broke and finish off both bottles. If I can't succeed at the basics of living, then why bother.

My attention is snapped back to the moment by an odd shape in a cornfield I pass on my way home. All the stalks were plowed down in the fall, so the ground should be flat. I slow down and squint as best I can through the blizzard. The shape is nearly covered with snow.

"Odd," I think and continue driving on to my apartment, which is set among a series of complexes on the other side of the cornfields. The bar-cornfield-apartment arrangement isn't all that uncommon in Wisconsin.

I pull into my parking lot, but can't get my mind off that unusual shape in the cornfield. It's cold and getting more miserable by the moment, and I want to get inside to my whiskey escape. Curiosity has the better of me, however, and I make a U-turn to return to the field a few hundred yards away. Slowly, I inch my car back, fishtailing in the deep and slippery snow. Reaching the edge of the field, I arrange my headlights to shed a dim light on the shape through the snow.

"OK," I think. "It's only something that got dumped there."

I put my car into reverse and as I turn my head to look behind me, I catch the shape twitch.

Sprinting to a stop, I quickly kneel next to the shape and brush off nearly an inch of snow. It's Chris, reeking of cigarettes, vodka and body odor. He's virtually unresponsive, blue, and cold to the touch. I slap him across the face a few times.

"Hey! Chris! Hey! Wake up!"

He moans and his eyes flutter open. Blearily, he tries to focus on me. Unexpectedly, he smiles.

"Thank you, Jesus. Thank you, Jesus," he slurs.

"Chris, I'm taking you to the hospital," I tell him as I pull his dirty and cold body off the ground and half-sling him over my shoulder.

"Thank you, Jesus," he says again. He stops and clutches me, staring at my face as best he can. "I'm looking at an angel."

"What?"

"I prayed to Jesus and he sent me an angel. He sent me an angel. You're an angel."

He slumps over me and I drag him to the car. Fortunately, the local hospital is not too far, and I have him to the emergency room within a few minutes. The nurses take him away on a stretcher as I hear him mumbling about angels.

The attending physician takes some quick notes as I recount how I found Chris. I laugh as I explain the town drunk thinks I'm an angel. The physician doesn't laugh.

"I don't know if you're an angel, but if you wouldn't have found him, I guarantee he would have died of exposure," he says.

"I'm sure someone else would have stopped for him," I say uncomfortably. He shakes his head.

"I've seen him in here a couple of times after he's been beaten up in bar fights. He's not the kind of guy people would go out of their way to help. You saved a life tonight. Don't take that lightly," he nods to me and leaves.

"I'm not man enough to talk to an angelic-looking girl, but the town drunk thinks I'm an angel," I think as I drive home.

I return to my apartment and make a cup of hot cocoa, looking outside to watch the snow bury the field where I found Chris. My thoughts turn to the unimbibed whiskey and codeine which remain entombed in their bottles. I wonder if I was indeed Chris's guardian angel or if he was actually mine.

NINETEEN

LEARNING A NEW LANGUAGE

Snow falls steadily outside the mostly steamed windows of Bruichladdich's still house. We are in the midst of our third snow day this week. On the first day, locals informed me that it never snows on Islay, so I should appreciate the rarity. On the second day, locals said snow on the island doesn't happen too often, so I should appreciate the rarity. On the third day, I stopped listening to the locals.

I pull open the window and peer outside, craning my neck around a couple of distillery buildings to look at the flakes fly over Loch Indaal. Bowmore, on the opposite side of the sea loch, has almost disappeared as the snow camouflages its whitewashed buildings. I can see faint coughs of vapor rising from the Bowmore Distillery steam stack, but they are quickly swallowed by the snow as well. The loch itself is raggedly choppy as the winter storm shoves the Atlantic against the rocky shore. A smattering of sea birds bounces miserably among the waves, unable to fly away even if they desperately wanted to escape. We are all trapped on this island, caged here.

The wind picks up, causing me to shudder. I shut the window and return my attention to the industrial action around me, praying to God that a machinery accident doesn't put me in need of life-or-death medical treatment from the inaccessible mainland on this wicked winter's day, because death would win.

Bruichladdich's still house is where the liquid "wash" that's been fermenting for days in the neighboring tun room comes to be transmogrified into whisky. Here, the wash is subjected to intense and repeated heat to be stripped of its immaturity and sharpened into an intense fighting spirit. This is where it learns to speak, to express itself, gaining the structure needed to communicate its essence to the world. The still house offers the best argument that alcohol is indeed the devil's device. It's hot as hell in here.

Watching over this process is another limper: Budgie, so-called because he chatters nonstop, like a singing budgie bird. His limp is more pronounced than Thomas's, and with the massive industrial equipment in here, it's easy to see how he could have obtained it. Like most men on the island, it's hard to tell how old he is, but I'd guess in his mid-forties. He has that spark in his eyes that tends to lead me in one direction with guessing his age, but growing up in the sea climate makes his wrinkles push my guess in the other direction. Something about him makes me think of the actor Armand Assante, with far less emoting, but just as much mystery.

"The monkey climbs where the devil dumps coal and chews the snake head," Budgie says in a trancelike croak. At least, that's what it sounds like he says.

Thomas was right when he warned me about Budgie's nonstop mouth, but he failed to adequately prepare me for the dual challenge of the roaring stills and Budgie's low mumble delivery. Budgie indeed has much to say, but I don't understand more than a fraction of his words. For the past few hours, I've followed him throughout the still house to help crank the gigantic valves and levers that dictate the flow of liquid and the temperatures at which the spirit is heated. Through it all, Budgie has been explaining to me what we're doing, invoking pagan chants or talking about his tractor, I'm not sure which.

"The army plants leave nothing but her porn," he emphatically states while pointing and looking at me, expectantly.

"The army plants leave nothing but her porn," he repeats, still seeming to expect a response. Suddenly, he walks in front of me and reaches for a lever, which he turns.

"That arm must be at a level where nothing will burn," he says again, and I finally understand. He wanted me to adjust a valve that monitors the heat level of the still so that we won't over-boil the wash.

The room's four gleaming copper stills rise more than twenty feet from base to the top of the neck, with the bulbous bases ranging from nearly ten feet wide to twelve feet wide, and the top of the neck narrowing to just over two feet in circumference. A flurry of pipes and valves surround the stills, and we methodically march between them, with Budgie's mystical mumblings leading the way.

Twelve thousand liters of wash are brought into the two wash stills first, where it is heated to temperatures as high as four hundred degrees Fahrenheit. As the liquid boils, the lighter alcohol vapors rise above the water and are funneled up the still neck. The neck of each still arches at a nearly ninety-degree angle to connect with a large condenser containing more than two hundred tiny copper tubes which cool the alcohol vapor into liquid for collection.

The first portion of spirits collected, the foreshots, is too strong for bottling – in fact it can be fatally strong – and is sent into a holding container to be redistilled. The "middle cut" is the portion that is kept for whisky and is captured when it is in the vicinity of 70 percent alcohol. The feints come out last. Here are the heavier, sulfurous impurities that also can be fatal, and they, too, are sent away to be redistilled.

I continue to do Budgie's bidding, paying more attention to his body language than to his incomprehensible instructions, which are eerily misinterpreted by my ears. Encouraging nods, perplexed scowls and his occasional physical placement of my hands on the proper device help me understand the basics of how these stills operate. Budgie shows extraordinary patience with me, and I deeply appreciate his calm demeanor and even tones. I think I'm coming across as only slightly more intelligent and capable than a partially deaf Dungeness crab when it comes to turning these levers the way he wants me to.

Budgie, on the other hand, has an innate ear for the stills that keeps him aware of their actions and effectiveness. He hears their cries when they say it's time to cool down, listens for their whines when they know there isn't enough liquid coming through, and eavesdrops on their whispers when they try to hold on to the liquid, refusing to let it pass through evenly. Most distilleries have left the traditional still man in the past, instead relying on a bank of computer measurements to dictate the still activity. Sure, a still man is there to push certain buttons at certain times, but they don't have the same guardian immediacy that Budgie provides the stills and their appendages. He is their confidant and translator.

I can't understand a word they're saying. To me, the intense boiling in the stills and passage of searing vapor through pipes sound like tortured screams. The wash bellows for relief and pleads to return to the quiet comfort of the fermentation tuns. This infernally forced maturity, the stripping of unwanted impurities, pounds the stills as relentlessly as a helpless soul wails to be released from hell. I wonder what screams are lost in these stills, and what screams this whisky will drown when it is finally drunk by people who live lonely in this world among those that don't bother to listen to them.

Everyone aches to be heard, no matter how scared they are of what people will think of their words. What do people think about me when I speak? Am I a weird, rambling mess of non sequiturs? Do I come across as thoughtful, intelligent and meaningful? Do my words have substance or are they like those foam peanuts in shipped packages – filling the space between to protect the fragility inside?

For well over half my life, I could barely speak with strangers. Mom's paranoia about crazy people drugging and kidnapping me really stuck. When I became a journalist, I had to change that. Paychecks wouldn't come if I didn't interview people for stories. The discomfort of this forced interaction was softened by my awareness of how difficult it is to speak with a stranger, both for me and the people I interviewed. I developed an ability to make interviewees feel exceedingly comfortable around me. It wasn't smoke and mirrors; I wasn't deliberately trying to relax them so I could pounce upon them and get otherwise unobtainable details. They found ways to be comfortable around me because I was trying just as hard to be comfortable around them.

As I grew as a journalist and then as a television writer and producer, I knew I did more than interview people as a means to earning a living. I was the ears that could listen to even the smallest life in the smallest moment. I gave other people a voice that I felt was never heard coming from my own mouth as a child.

*

Budgie laughs as he finishes whatever story he was telling, and I offer a supportive chuckle, though I was lost in my own silent monologue and not listening. We are like these huge boiling pots surrounding us: distilling our own thoughts through our minds and out our mouths over and over, hoping to refine our own essences into something the angels accept and humans want.

TWENTY

ROBBIE BURNS AND ROBBY BREAKS

Scotland's most holy night is this weekend, and I am getting away to enjoy the reverence, sacred texts and heavenly music. Well, at least that's one positive way to spin it. Saturday is actually the annual Burns Supper, a drunken revelry of impassioned poetry, gut-busting food and raucous music that celebrates Scotland's national literary hero, Robert Burns. His works extol the virtues of Scottish life, whisky and the lands that are the cradle of both.

The family who own the cottage I'll return to after leaving the distillery has invited me to join them for the weekend on a journey to the Isle of Jura for a celebration of Burns' 250th birthday. I'm to join Dylan and his wife Rachel, their charming teenage daughter Megan, sporty son Connor and youngest daughter whose beautiful Gaelic name I can't pronounce, let alone spell. Our trip gets off to an inauspicious start as I slip into the front seat to ride shotgun with Dylan. Rachel and the kids stare at me as I shut the passenger door and settle into my seat to wait for Dylan to lock the house. The hushed stares are finally broken by Rachel.

"Are...you...planning on driving?" she hesitantly asks.

I look forward and see the steering wheel a foot in front of me. I say a quiet prayer that one day I'll be able to remember on which side the driver sits and which side the passenger sits in these backwards UK vehicles. I answer Rachel with a negative and exit the car to move to the passenger side of the vehicle. Dylan slides into the driver's seat, and we make the short drive to the Jura ferry.

Though it's before 5:00 p.m., the sun has been gone for over an hour, making the passage seem even more adventurous. Crossing the Sound to get to Islay's stark and imposing island neighbor only takes a few minutes. Despite the ferry's strong engines, I feel uneasy as we make the brief trip. The engines work to fight across every inch of the fast-flowing Sound, which shoots beneath us at 25 knots. Rachel is even less optimistic than me. She's standing outside the vehicle, waiting to grab a life jacket and jump overboard if the ship falls victim to the strong current.

Jura has fewer than two hundred residents, none of them on the ferry-terminal side of the island, so the uninhabited hills are brooding shadows as the ferry reaches the Jura pier. Dylan follows the lead of the other ten drivers on the tightly packed ferry and fires up the Land Rover. Like an expeditionary force, we slowly leave the ferry one-by-one in search of our evening's quarry: drink and dance.

Our caravan makes the eight-mile drive down a narrow, winding road to the small village of Craighouse, and Dylan deftly dodges dozens of red deer that dart in front of his truck. With no predators and little development on the island, there are some eight thousand deer that roam freely. This time of night, they are returning from their daily foraging along the coast where they relish dining on seaweed that washes onto the shore after every high tide.

Distilling Rob: Manly Lies and Whisky Truths

We arrive at Jura's only hotel, which is where we're staying for the night. The nineteenth century building is tidy and compact, with perhaps a dozen rooms. Each room has its own washbasin with a communal bathroom in the hallway. Our "family" occupies a small wing of the hotel, allowing us privacy from other guests. Though, it seems Dylan knows everyone else in the hotel, so it's not like we're amongst strangers, other than me.

Dylan and thirteen-year-old Connor are clad in kilts. This is one of the few occasions Scottish men have to wear their kilts. In stark contrast to their three-hundred-year-old throwback outfits are Rachel and her daughters, who all wear jeans and smart tops. Burns Supper is for everyone, but the boys are the ones that get to play dress-up for it.

I'm really taking the stag by the horns with my attire tonight. I want to announce loudly and boldly that I am not from here. I am the American who has retreated to these wild lands in an attempt to tame my aimlessly wandering soul. Most of the clothes I've brought to Islay are functional cargo pants and t-shirts. Things I would wear to clean the apartment back in LA, but never out, not even to the grocery store. A trip to pick up toilet paper would require three outfit changes before I walked out the door feeling comfortable. You can never be caught looking less than your best in LA. Those who do are quickly exiled to decidedly unfashionable places like Encino and Long Beach. I've brought one outfit with me to carry that attitude across the world.

Tonight, I am wearing a tailored black jacket, cashmere turtleneck, designer jeans, Bruno Magli loafers, and L.A. Eyeworks glasses. In all, I'm probably clad in some fifteen-hundred-dollars worth of clothing and accessories. In many ways, I've definitely outgrown those days of wanting to hide outside of a circle. Now I want the circle to form around me where awestruck men will buy me drinks and breathless women will give me whatever I desire. Yes, I'm sporting my James Bond attitude tonight, and I'm hoping it's vibrant enough to distract people from the fact that I'm worried about what they'll think of an American crashing this Scottish cultural treasure.

We all head downstairs to the hotel's small bar for some pre-festivity drinks. The bar is crowded with other visitors from Islay, as well as quite a few locals. I walk in, expecting to be deluged with questions and stares about who this mysterious man is. Instead, the only people who will chat with me are Dylan's children and even they don't seem all that interested in talking to this old man dressed in black whose breath is beginning to reek of whisky and beer. This is far from the dream of people flocking to meet a suave superspy with sangfroid command of his surroundings that I am trying for tonight.

Men lean elbow-to-elbow against the small wooden bar ordering cheap pints, and women holding wine glasses congregate in an alcove. I collect my diminishing ego and try to strike up conversations with different people around me. The bar is too loud and their interest too short for the chats to lead anywhere. Plus, any conversation I initiate in this environment sends both of us straining to make out each other's accents. Mercifully, the Burns Supper is starting soon and we begin an orderly retreat from the pub to the village hall down the street. As we gather ourselves, Dylan hands me a case of beer that he purchased from the bartender and asks me to carry it down to the dinner hall. It's a Burns BYOB.

I pick up the box by the handle holes and notice they feel a little soggy. In fact, the entire box feels quite moist, and I momentarily wonder how the wet cardboard can support the weight of all these bottles.

CRASH.

The bottom falls out of the box. I feel the mushy cardboard give way and try to dance my legs around to block and minimize the damage to the falling bottles. Instead, I end up kicking several all over the room. One bottle smashes against a table, another against the bar. Two explode at my feet. I am soaked in suds. At least I finally have my wish. Everyone is paying attention to me.

"Bloody Americans!" one man laughs.

"Told you Americans can't handle their liquor," shouts another.

"You're supposed to drink beer, Yank, not piss it away!" the oldest man in the bar chimes in.

"I don't like America," a young boy whispers to his mother. "Except when they helped us in World War Two."

"At least we have Obama!" I blurt out before I do any more damage to America's reputation.

The mood immediately shifts. Dylan grabs a towel to wipe me down, and another man brings a solid box for the remaining beers.

"Obama gave me hope for America," a woman says, wiping some beer from her own legs.

"Americans finally see they need to fix the mess they've made," a man offers.

"Do you think he really makes a difference?" another person asks.

I'm deluged with questions about Obama and whether or not he can lead Americans back to the Promised Land as world leaders. He's been in office less than a month. We're still fighting two wars and I hear more and more stories from friends and family back home about their job losses and financial woes. I don't know if he's ever going to solve those problems, but he just saved me from an international crisis.

We walk down the street to the village hall, kilt-clad men and one wet American. My Italian loafers squish out beer with each step, but as I answer people's questions about why I'm on the islands, my previous life in LA, my ideas about how Obama can help my country regain its balance, I realize at this moment I'm happier being a wet Rob than a dry James Bond.

TWENTY-ONE

PURGING THE IMPURITIES

"I was gutted. I couldn't think straight. I still can't. My mind is thinking all the time and it seems...turn that lever and lower the heat in the spirit still... I can't believe he's gone and just like that. I'm still broken up by it and I'm not myself at all," Budgie says as we move between the stills.

All morning we've alternated between monitoring the still production and cleaning every nook and cranny we can find. The reason for the cleaning is unclear, but it seems something big is afoot. Maybe Jim McEwan has finally returned from his travels and the place needs to be in tip-top shape for his inspection. I hope that's the case. I'm getting increasingly anxious about finally getting some time alone with him to hear his lifelong battle stories in the whisky industry and how it's made him into the man he is today. Instead of hearing whisky wisdom from Jim, I've been having a much more personal talk with Budgie, the kind that makes you want to stop everything and sit down with a whisky in your hand to give the subject the full attention it deserves.

"It happened up the road from here. I still can't believe it," Budgie continues. "Died after swerving to avoid a cow and smashed into a lorry. I'm not myself. I came into work the next day, but they made me go home and take some time off. My own brother, gone."

Now several days into working together, my ears have adjusted to Budgie's accented mumble amidst the roar of machinery. He's talked a lot about his brother the past couple of days. This week marks a month since the fatal accident, which happened less than a mile from the distillery.

"I won't ever drive past that spot again without thinking of my brother," Budgie says.

We've been talking a lot about life in the last day, and about death. He shares stories about his brother, and I hesitantly open the door to my own helpless loss by sharing stories about my cousin Brian, who's now been dead longer than he was alive. I was just out of college when he was killed in a car accident two days after getting his license at age sixteen.

I took the call from my Aunt Sharon on a hot August evening while making dinner in my parents' kitchen. She said friends of Brian had called. They were following his car as it raced down a country road when he left the pavement and slammed into a tree. Things didn't look good.

We sprang into action, albeit robotically. Mom and Dad went to my aunt's while I raced to the accident scene. There, crushed against a lone oak tree along a bean field, the only tree for two hundred feet in either direction, was my cousin's hand-me-down car. A large hole in the windshield showed where his passenger, his best friend, had ejected to his death. An ambulance was getting ready to pull away when I arrived; inside was Brian. I took it as a miraculous sign that he would survive, because the car looked like death itself; yet, he was pulled out alive.

Distilling Rob: Manly Lies and Whisky Truths

Twelve hours later, my aunt and uncle made the decision to take him off life support. His life hadn't been ideal – full of run-ins with police, school principals and anyone else he could piss off. Now, it was over and the amends he'd recently promised to make would never be fulfilled.

There, facing my family, in an abrupt and ugly manner, was death. But, within that death there was also rebirth and redemption.

My dad, whose relationship with his sister was difficult in the best of times, suddenly stood stronger, firmer and braver; different than I'd ever seen him. His father had become a dependable patriarch after he stopped drinking. Now, in this time of sorrow, Dad gently and confidently took that mantle from Grandpa.

Dad made the funeral arrangements, paid expenses out of his own pocket, and pledged his devotion to his sister and her husband, promising to be a better brother and brother-in-law. He held the family tight so the rest of us could let go.

He was almost like the spirit that pumps through the stills surrounding me: it comes in with a complex background that needs to be gradually refined until the impurities are purged. After it passes through the heat enough times, it is ready to take its first step toward standing on its own, strong and transparent. Dad had made it past his troubling childhood, Vietnam and the Gulf War, a lifetime of underpaid and undervalued jobs, and the tumultuous ride of inescapable fatherhood to finally live firmly as his own man.

I wrap up telling Budgie about Dad's transformation.

"I wish my cousin would have been able to have that kind of rebirth," I say and point to the stills. "It's like this spirit being boiled over and over until it finally reaches its full potential, you know?"

"No," Budgie says, shaking his head. "That's whisky. What you're talking about is living long enough to live right."

"Aye," I nod and shrug. "Your brother, he lived right?"

"Aye. Aye," Budgie moves to adjust the temperature of the still. "That he did."

TWENTY-TWO

SHADOWS IN THE MOONSHINE

I finally know why we spent yesterday cleaning every grime-coated pipe and tarnished copper surface in sight. BBC Alba, the BBC's Gaelic TV station, is in the still house today to do a piece about Bruichladdich. Distillery Manager Duncan speaks Gaelic fluently and embraces the opportunity to describe the distillery in the beautiful ancient tongue of his island. Bruichladdich is no stranger to media attention. They milk every angle possible to shine the spotlight on the distillery. If there is such a thing as being gimmicky without being gimmicky, they do it here.

The TV crew, Budgie and I do a delicate dance around the still house equipment. I smile as Budgie and the cameraman politely but persistently jockey for position so they can each do their jobs. I've been working in here long enough to know that most of the "work" Budgie is doing at the moment is unnecessary. He doesn't really need to turn that valve or test the alcohol strength of that still. I'm not sure if he's maintaining his position so he can be captured on camera or if he's adamantly asserting dominance over his domain. Duncan gives Budgie a quizzical look as the still man walks across the middle of an establishing shot for no apparent reason.

"Budgie, why don't you give the stills one more clean?" Duncan suggests.

Budgie mumbles, well, actually he's been mumbling this entire time, but this time he actually mumbles in relation to something that matters and agrees with Duncan's suggestion. Despite our efforts yesterday, the copper stills collect deposits of minerals, dust and who knows what else on a daily basis. Budgie applies oil that keeps them clean, but more importantly, conditions the copper in an attempt to extend the lives of the stills.

As Budgie swabs oil over the stills that are outside of camera shot, I make my way to the nearest window. The heat from the camera crew's lights has improbably jacked up the temperature in the still house even higher than normal. It's the first week of February and the outside temperature is freezing, though there is no sign in the skies of more of the rare snow that has come regularly this year. As I let the cool outside air wash over my boiling boiler suit, I'm tempted to lean outside and touch a palm tree.

Islay, like Ireland and much of the western UK, finds that more than just temperate air makes the journey along the Gulf Stream from warmer places. Plants that are normally seen far, far away from this part of the world occasionally pop up here, especially palm trees. They're small and wispy compared to truly tropical palm trees, but they give an impression of warmth when none is to be found.

I can no longer resist the temptation. I reach out and stroke one of the palm fronds. Definitely chillier than the ones I'm used to in LA. Yet, there's a familiarity with it that takes me far away from Islay.

Distilling Rob: Manly Lies and Whisky Truths

*

A full moon bobs between the fronds of a sixty-foot palm tree that rises above the driveway across from my second-story apartment window. Maybe the moon isn't bobbing as much as my eyes are. I'm camped in front of a clunker of a computer in my sparse bedroom, surfing the Internet to make the hours go by. I look down at the thirty-two-ounce plastic McDonald's cup that has become my nightly companion. It was completely filled with two pounds of a homemade Long Island Ice Tea, but half of that is gone. Now that I think about it, this is the second one I've had tonight. That means I've already had six, no eight, no ten...math was never my strong suit. I've had a lot of shots tonight. I stick a nail-less index finger into the icy drink and give it a swirl.

The fingernail came off a month ago, which was nearly two months after I slammed my finger into the door of my Ford Explorer, which was nearly an hour after I'd arrived in LA. Well, closer to three, as I first had to drive two hours past strip malls and chain stores stretching from the San Bernardino Mountains to my apartment on the Westside, close to Santa Monica. The broken finger was the highlight of my first twenty-four hours in LA. By the following evening, I'd totaled my truck, found out my mom's dad was hospitalized with a stroke, and the girl I'd fallen madly in love with back home told me she was in love with someone else. Welcome to Hollywood.

I'd left Wisconsin overflowing with hope and confidence, as many people who come to LA do. My accolades in television in the Midwest, winning national awards for the travel show I wrote and directed, were enough for me to dream that I would find success in the land of my childhood heroes, write some brilliant screenplays, win lots of awards and make loads of money. Besides, I had reached the point in Wisconsin where I needed to commit to a life there (unmarried in your mid-twenties means the gay rumors fly like the December snow, so you'd better find a wife soon) and settle for good, or I had to make my boldest attempt yet to break away from the gravitational crawl of my hometown.

By the time that miserable first day in LA had passed, the newly nurtured hope and confidence that I could make something of myself, not just here, but in life, had evaporated. As the days and weeks went by, I was scared to leave the apartment and terrified to drive again. The faded sun that wearily crept through the smog-induced perma-haze and into my dingy bedroom made my life feel darker. Warm temperatures that I'd dreamed of enjoying when I was freezing in Wisconsin turned my airless apartment into a sauna. Into a hell.

Three months after I saw my apartment for the first time, I sit alone, drunk. I haven't found television work. I haven't found any work. My savings is nearing the bottom thanks to the aforementioned lack of work and the car wreck. Much of the little money I have goes to revive the numbing inebriation I weaned myself from the past year in Wisconsin when my life started to improve. I don't feel ashamed about this spirit retreat; I feel defeated. My shame comes from the other desperate distraction I've brought into my life.

There's a knock on at the front door. I put down the super-size Long Island Ice Tea and pick up a bottle of tequila sitting next to my bed. I chug a mouthful as I walk to the living room to answer the knock. If I do have any trace of self-worth left, it's best to neutralize it before I open the door. My complete lack of work and money has allowed me to do only two things beside drink: write a spec screenplay and experiment with this new thing in LA called Internet dating. It's really not even dating. You look at a grainy picture of a stranger and read the uninformative two-sentence blurb they added about themselves and ask to meet them. Marginally better than hitting on someone at the grocery store and significantly less humiliating if you're rejected.

The knuckles rapping on the other side of the door belong to one of these Internet girls. I try to steady my balance as I approach the door and struggle to remember which one she is. I think we've met before. It doesn't matter. I'm sure that like with all the other girls I meet online our emails have been practically pornographic; like all the others she wasn't particularly interesting; and like all the others she wouldn't be very attractive. I was less than nobody in LA and hadn't yet learned to lie about that fact (which is the standard way of life in LA), which meant I had zero shot with anyone attractive. Instead, I ended up with the kind of woman I wouldn't even look at back home. And I'm sure on the other side of the door is a woman who is thinking about all she left behind to pursue her hopes and dreams, and now agonizes over how she ended up with someone like me: boozed out, broke and emotionally bereft.

One more swig and I open the door. There's my Internet date: short, stout, not dressed well and wearing a look of disappointed desperation that probably mirrors mine. She glances at the bottle in my hand and forces a smile. I remember which one she is. We've had three "dates." Our first was to a matinee movie and then back to her place. Our last two have been to my bedroom.

"Hey," I slur with all the suaveness a "hey" deserves and invite her into my prison for our conjugal visit.

We walk past the outdoor patio furniture that makes up the dining room, the cardboard boxes that bookend my tattered couch and the cracked ice cooler where the rabbit-eared TV sits. Ths is what my one-hundred-thousand-dollar college education has gotten me: a home worse than the ones I swore I'd never live in back in Beloit.

"I brought limes," she whispers in an attempt to be seductive, but we both know our time together isn't worthy of seduction and her words are said only half-heartedly.

The limes are meant to complement the tequila. We're co-opting what should be a very sexy foreplay tool, body shots, as a means to get us through what will inevitably happen. Ideally, body shots heighten the tension of the slow and eager removal of clothes as you playfully lick salt and lime off each other followed by a shot of tequila. For me, body shots increasingly blur my mind with each article of clothing she takes off so I can block out my once chivalrous vision of giving myself emotionally and physically only to my "soul mate." Now, I desperately want to sense someone else's touch, anyone's touch, so I will feel something in this nothingness.

I hit the remote on my CD player as the girl bounces on my bed. The Rolling Stones' *Exile on Main Street* kicks in, a soundtrack for someone who feels like an exile in his own bedroom. What follows is a blur of lime slices, cheap clothing, cheap tequila and the slapping of skin on skin. We ache so much with our sad loneliness that we spend our isolation miserably together.

"Harder, harder!" she pleads. "Fuck me angry!"

I do. I fuck her angry. I fuck her with the resentment of lost loves and broken hearts. I fuck her like all the beatings a child takes for not being good enough. We fuck like we hate each other and we fuck like we hate ourselves. We do. All her screaming and all my slapping are nothing more than amplified whimpers for help. We're scared of being alone and even more scared to admit it.

Distilling Rob: Manly Lies and Whisky Truths

Though my mind spins with alcohol and animal ecstasy, I can't help but picture her, this virtual stranger, as a little girl wanting to make her parents proud enough to love her. Someone's daughter who has ended up trapped with me for a night: a little boy who has wandered too far from the safety of his Wisconsin home. But, I don't belong there. I don't belong here. It's hard to belong anywhere when you don't have a sense of even belonging in your own body.

*

"You thinking of home?" Budgie asks, nodding toward the palm tree. In the course of my frond-induced time travel, he's finished polishing the stills and the camera crew is breaking down their equipment.

"Budgie, my friend," I say as I gesture to the distillery, "this is the only home I have."

TWENTY-THREE

WHERE NOBODY KNOWS MY NAME

The Lochindaal pub has become my regular retreat; though, the real regulars here stare at me like a stray cat they've gotten used to having around but still won't adopt. I walk through the door and heads lift up from drinks, conversations drop slightly and eyes follow me to the wobbly stool that's become my perch. I nod to a perpetually sloshed middle-aged woman who has tried to pick up on me half a dozen times, mutually ignore her equally drunk, de facto boyfriend, and give a small wave to a white-haired horse trainer who grunts out a slight retort.

My shoes have a brief struggle to lift off the sticky floor as I sit on the stool. Instinctively, I reach my left hand to the bar top to steady the inevitable counter-rock the uneven stool will boomerang in response to my weight. Wood creaks beneath my butt and the chair shudders, but holds. The last thing I need is to break something in here and be put on Matty's blacklist, forever banned from the one haven I've found.

The frenetic cook/bartender dashes between the bar and the kitchen, which is located outside, across the alley. A work crew is here from the mainland for the week to add new cables to the island's telecommunication lines, so Matty actually has people to cook for aside from me. I have no idea how long I'll wait for him to pay attention to me. My mind is elsewhere, anyway.

Before I set foot on the ferry that took me to Islay, I'd pictured an island "Brigadoon" where I would be uplifted high enough to see my true place in the world. I believed that the longer I was here, the more the magic would sweep me away, and I'd be embraced by natives as one of their own. That hasn't happened. I'm more of a tolerated curiosity than a trusted compatriot.

Today was my last day working with Budgie. I'm still not sure if I totally understand what he says, and I don't know if my stories perk his ears half as much as the rumble of the stills, but he's grown on me. Sharing the bond of close family loss transcends any conversation we may have; but, in truth, we've been nothing more than passing strangers. I walked out of the steaming still house for the last time this evening and into the cold feeling as foreign as the day I stepped off the ferry.

"You look like a boy who's thinking hard there, Robbie," Matty says as he finally pours me a Famous Grouse mixed with lemonade. They don't have soda here, which is my normal way of drowning a mediocre blended Scotch, so I settle for this acceptable alternative.

"Matty, I am thinking hard," I respond. I point to a bottle of Budweiser and nod to him. It's his favorite beer, and he opens it eagerly. Tipping isn't big here, but buying drinks for the bartender is.

"What's the thinking about?"

"I came here to try to find some direction for my life. Figure *something* out. But, all I keep doing is thinking about the past. I thought I'd find answers here. Inspiration. But, I honestly don't see anything."

"Yes, yes. I see the problem. I see," he nods with a rapid jerk. "Don't look!"

"How do you mean?"

"If you're going to see something, you're going to see it. If you're not, you're not. Don't look, it doesn't matter. Either you will or you won't. You see?" he expounds as he takes a swig and winks. "Whatcha looking for, anyway?"

"I'm trying to figure my life out and see what it means to be a man," I reply and grasp how ridiculous that sounds as soon as it leaves my mouth.

"Oh, Jesus Christ! Why in heavens are you doing that?"

"You've lived a big life, traveled around the world. When did you stop and think to yourself, 'Now I'm a man?'"

He snorts so loudly, three women playing pool stop to check out the sound.

"If brains were dynamite, I wouldn't have enough to blow my nose," he declares emphatically and walks away with his staccato laugh trailing behind him.

"What the hell's that supposed to mean, Matty?" I shout out after him. He goes around a corner, still laughing. "What's that supposed to mean?!?"

Great. I'm in a dive bar, being mocked by a crazy cook. I've traveled halfway around the world to find some divine truth about adulthood in the seemingly manly whisky industry, and so far I've worked with one guy who won't speak, another who won't shut up, and neither of them drinks much whisky. More time has been spent standing around aimlessly than doing any actual work. Any slight financial benefit I may be getting from my time at the distillery is going straight to my liver. In the one month I've been on the island, I've made no friends aside from the aforementioned crazy cook.

My debts are piling up as my life savings rapidly goes down. I'm paying $250 a month to have my stuff stuffed into a storage unit. My dog hates me for sticking her in the cargo hold of a plane and taking her out of warm LA for my parents' place in frigid Wisconsin. I've been wearing the same four shirts for weeks. I'm living on an island where the men are men and the single women are nonexistent. There is no goddamn Mexican food within five thousand miles!

I slam my drink on the bar. The resulting splatter slaps my face back to the moment. One of the pool-playing women has moved to the bar in the midst of my internal rant. She offers me a napkin, and I dab the sour residue off my face.

I drop a handful of pound coins on the bar and pull back the stool. I'm in no mood to stay. Tomorrow I start working in the warehouse at Bruichladdich. I pray I won't be standing around doing nothing.

TWENTY-FOUR

CASK STRENGTH

I never thought I'd say this, but at the moment, I'm having trouble handling my whisky. I can feel it backing up on me. Perhaps I should have said no to the Scotch that was offered to me instead of trying to prove that I'm a...

"Be a man!" a teasing, yet cheering voice shouts from behind me.

Gritting my teeth, I take a deep breath and...heave. The whisky cask settles into place without crashing into the wall. Aaron, who moves casks for a living, gives me an encouraging nod.

I wipe a stream of sweat from my forehead and tap my hard hat in response to Aaron. My wish has come true. I am definitely not standing around without purpose. I have just finished rolling a ton of whisky across a warehouse floor with only my strength and the ancient ingenuity of cask design to assist me.

Casks have been around since long before Christ. History has forgotten who first thought of creating a hollow wooden vessel to transport food, wine and other items, but they were brilliant. Modern casks use the same designs as in ancient times, with wooden staves shaped and tempered to create a bulging middle and two tapered ends. The tapering allows the cask to be rocked back and forth, rolled with precision around corners, spun in place and pretty much moved any way a person wants to move it. The genius in this design is it allows one person to move massive weights that would take ten men to lift.

Like other distilleries, Bruichladdich uses casks that range between 30 liters, 190 liters, 250 liters, and 500 liters. Most of the casks are reused bourbon casks, but a decent number are reused sherry casks and a variety of wine casks, including a kosher wine from Israel. In this little cask world the feisty new spirit goes off to school and gains character under the tutelage of the former liquid the cask previously held. It's a wonderful self-contained universe where spirit, wood and air come together for the slow process that ends with Scotch whisky. Here is where that young spirit matures into its adult self.

I am inside a massive warehouse with upwards of twenty-five thousand casks stacked in racks as high as sixty feet above the floor. The walls and floor are gray and cheerless, made darker by a minimal amount of lighting. The entire building is filled with the sweet aroma of whisky and wood. The warehouse is unheated, which allows the whisky to age at a steady pace throughout the years, as even in the summer months the temperature doesn't significantly rise in the warehouse. On this winter morning, I'm glad to be moving casks, for even as I wipe the sweat from my brow I see a faint frosty mist form in front of my face with each breath.

"Bloody hell," says a matter-of-fact voice next to me. I turn and look up at Jack, who stands nearly a half-foot taller than my 6 feet 1 frame. "Who was the fucking genius who said we needed to move the last fucking cask in the row to another bloody rack? Do they have any fucking idea how much effort this takes?"

"Well, we can fairly readily surmise who said, off the top of their head, this would be no problem without actually thinking about what the challenges were," responds Aaron, who is at least a foot shorter than Jack.

"Aye," Jack calmly agrees while contemplating the work before us. "Well, he can fucking come down here and move the bloody things himself."

Aaron and Jack, both in their twenties, are the warehouse boys that I have been helping all morning and will continue to help for the foreseeable future. Both returned to Islay after going away to the mainland for university and eventually found themselves working at the distillery. Jack, tall and thin with prematurely graying hair, still has a baby face, and his easygoing voice doesn't match the frustration in his words. Aaron, with blondish hair and a freshly started Fu-Manchu mustache, is handsome in a TV-actor kind of way, and based on many of the stars I'd met in Hollywood, his stature is equal to theirs. His Scottish accent is rounded with the English tones of his parents, who were immigrants to Islay when he was a child.

We are in the midst of removing eight casks from a row to retrieve a single cask. The job is to move this single cask to another part of the warehouse because...well, we're not really sure of the reasoning. Ours is not to question why. There are still four more casks to move to reach the vessel that needs to be stored elsewhere, and then we have to put everything back. At least this is a ground-level rack. The racks reach to the ceiling and doing this task up there would require a mechanical lift and a lot of up-and-down activity.

"If you guys want, I could drink the whisky out of the casks blocking the one we need, which would make them a lot easier to move," I offer.

"Brilliant!" Aaron perks up. "We can put a chair against the wall for you, set up a hose from the cask to your mouth. Minimal effort for you, really."

"Well, if you're going to do that, I'm going to the fucking pub for a few pints until you finish," Jack states. "I've earned it."

"I have faith in you, Rob. If we leave you alone, I believe you can finish off these casks by, oh, let's say four o'clock? We can come back for an hour and then move the cask to its new rack and call it a day," adds Aaron, as though it's a done deal.

"Fuck that, I'm staying at the pub all day," Jack affirms.

We all share a laugh and get back to the casks before us. Aaron wedges his way between the narrow rows and Jack bends in half at the end of the row to receive the cask Aaron sends his way. Jack swivels the cask and gives it a shove my way. The massive container wobbles down the uneven cement floor toward me. I time my reach to slow the cask before it gets too much momentum to be manageable and then I roll it further down the main aisle. Despite the ingenious design, controlling the cask still takes tremendous effort and concentration. One lapse of focus and slip of a hand to the side of the cask could result in broken bones or severed finger if the vessel pins your hand against a wall, as I've been told more than once.

An hour later, the single cask is moved, the originals are put back in place. As we walk to our next cask-moving task, I smile to myself. For the first time since I started working at the distillery, I actually feel like I'm directly connected with the whisky and with the job. I also sense I am part of the team.

Distilling Rob: Manly Lies and Whisky Truths

One of the guys. Aaron and Jack are a decade younger than me, but our bond is forged in approach and attitude rather than age. They are laid-back and loose-spirited guys, which is the opposite of most of my work peers in the political world. I'm happy here.

I stop myself. I *am* happy here, hanging with guys who have the kind of jobs I wanted to sprint away from when I was growing up. I try to analyze why that is, but deliberately pull back the reins of my introspective high horse. I don't want to compare now to then; these guys in Scotland to those guys in Wisconsin; manual labor to my office jobs; or boys to men. I am happy here and now. I'm going to let myself enjoy that feeling and be present in it.

"You know you can feel free to get your arse over here to help us," Jack says, bringing me out of my head and getting my legs moving again. I flash a quick smile and nod.

"I'm glad you're smiling," he says. "I thought you might think I was really upset."

"I don't care if you were," I respond. "I'm just happy to be here."

"Christ, you are?" he says incredulously.

I stop again and consider.

"Yes. I am."

My smile leads the way to the next row of casks we have to move.

TWENTY-FIVE

THE MALLEABILITY OF TIME

Perfect moments. A woman saying "I do" to a proposal? Seeing the birth of a child? Scoring the winning goal in overtime to win the Stanley Cup? I've never experienced anything as grand as those happenings. For me, a perfect moment is something that seems small to the outside world, but is huge inside your world. Chatting with your best friends on a lakeshore, fishing pole in one hand and a Scotch in the other; dancing with your prom date and feeling like you truly belong on the floor with her; getting a free second go-round on a rollercoaster with a group of college friends because the operator had so much fun watching you shriek with delight the first time; or blowing your vocal cords out singing at the top of your lungs halfway through a twenty-hour cross-country drive as you chase the sinking sun.

Right now, I'm having a perfect moment. I sit in a chair on the front lawn of the distillery guesthouse on this unseasonably warm winter's night. Granted, I'm still wearing a thermal cap and a winter jacket, but at least I can sit out here without the threat of rain, wind that will blow me to the still house or cold that will turn my nose brittle. The moon, rarely seen the past few weeks due to clouds, seems close enough to touch and lights up Loch Indaal, turning it into an incandescent elixir. I'm sipping a dram of 16 year-old Bruichladdich aged in a bourbon cask, and it dances across my palate like a crème brûlée glazed with caramelized sugar and topped with fresh fruit.

People often ask me what my favorite whisky is. I tell them, in all honesty, it's whatever whisky you're drinking when you realize you're having a perfect moment. A whisky that is perhaps dull in one situation suddenly takes on new significance if you're sharing it with Nepalese river guides along the Ganges after an intense day of whitewater rafting in India. It goes from plain to perfect. The Bruichladdich I have tonight is already pretty close to perfect, and it's only better with the atmosphere.

I'm aching after another full day of moving casks. Despite the ease with which they move considering their size, the constant hunching over and the effort needed to get them rolling and then stop them has long-dormant muscles complaining. Right now, the whisky and the crisp air give those muscles a chance to relax and allow my mind to break away from the repetitive recollection of today's rolling, rolling, rolling.

Being alone on an island provides an interesting lesson in the malleability of time. Personal time, historical time, world time – they all fluctuate at intervals that fall outside of linear time. At the moment, the world's panic over economics and epidemics is whizzing by me so rapidly I can barely capture the issues with a thought. Historical time is moving as slowly as the moon over the loch, with a nearby five-thousand-year-old standing stone serving as a reminder that for epochs people have pondered life under the same reflected light as I am in this very spot. My personal time is once again taking me away from the present and sending me back to another full moon, another whisky in hand and another perfect moment.

*

I had no money. Nothing. Enough to last one more week in LA, at best. Then I'd have to beg my parents for gas cash so I could make the long, demoralizing retreat to Wisconsin and surrender to the bleak existence I'd temporarily escaped. Less than a year of struggling in LA threatened to erase a lifetime spent getting here. Temp jobs, though with intriguing places like Disney Studios or Creative Artists Agency, failed to materialize into anything long term. I'd taken to skulking through nearby malls in semi-disguise to get chosen to participate in random market research surveys. I would lie about my age, my demographic, whatever was needed to clear the screening process. I once pulled off a Hispanic man in his fifties. I think the surveyor was more interested in his quota than the truth that particular day. Surveys paid up to ten dollars an interview and some included a coupon for a free Cinnabon. I'd become a pastry grifter.

This was a Band-Aid approach to financial survival that couldn't sustain me. When my bank account bottomed to the point where I had to leave LA or become homeless, I answered the type of classified ad I'd avoided for the better part of a year. The position was for a newspaper editor, and I'd sworn I'd never go back to journalism again. Ever. Ever... Desperate times...

I don't know if it was fate, divine intervention or the luck of the Irish, but within the course of one week, I'd gone from being on the verge of crawling away from LA in defeat to being named the managing editor of a large community newspaper in the Hollywood and Beverly Hills area.

The search for the personal identity I'd been missing since I left Wisconsin finally found a measure of worth within me thanks to the job. I could look out my office window every day and see the legendary Hollywood sign. I could stroll down Melrose Avenue for lunch and pass by movie stars who were out shopping. I could tell people I was somebody: a newspaper editor in Hollywood.

Instead of being so socially awkward and unwanted that every night was spent drinking alone at home, I found myself invited to celebrity-packed Hollywood parties, art gallery openings, launches of new bars and restaurants, and frequently all of them in the course of a single evening. I finally had an external structure to wrap myself with some self-confidence. Gone were the desperate women who randomly came to me as their sad last resort. They were replaced by aspiring actresses and models whose interest in me was only minimally more genuine, but who were more than willing to have the chance to interact with Hollywood's elite as my guest at these events. It was a classier form of mutual use than drunken Internet hookups: I had the companionship of the kind of beautiful women I could once only see on TV; they had access to scenes where they could be seen and "discovered."

Somewhere between the self-loathing life of unemployment and the self-consuming life of Hollywood, I tried to unite who I was inside with what I had outside. For the first time, I realized that all those years of inching forward (and then falling back) had left me with small but solid footholds within my ego. As low as I'd sunken with my nights of debauchery, perhaps lower than I'd even been in my life, I also knew I was able to climb out of those spaces to a higher perch than I ever had. For once, I was starting to feel that I wasn't hiding behind external success, but that I actually deserved it.

Distilling Rob: Manly Lies and Whisky Truths

I'd only been on the newspaper job for a couple of months when my publisher assigned me to do a feature on two young women who were trying to make it big in the LA opera scene. There wasn't anything particularly newsworthy about them. Hundreds, if not thousands of young opera singers struggle to make it in LA every day. The difference with these two is they had paid cash to place an advertisement in my paper to find students to tutor (they were struggling singers who needed some way to earn money, after all), and they were quite pretty. Money and beauty were primary factors my publisher often used in issuing editorial directives.

Interacting with a journalist is a professional encounter that makes most people nervous. When you go to the dry cleaner, have an exterminator come to your home or listen to a park ranger, you generally don't become self-conscious and wonder if you're coming across as intelligent or if the dry cleaner will twist your words and starch when you insist she not. When someone sits across from a journalist, reactions range from distrust to fear, but usually people just want to please. As a journalist who started out dreadfully shy, the intimidation my profession provided certainly worked to my advantage. It's hard for people to notice how nervous you are sitting across from them when they're even more nervous being across from you.

Rosella and Chloe were giddy, apprehensive and unconditionally wanting to please when I interviewed them in their cluttered music room. Both were dark-haired hotties, smart, funny and kind. Their anxious energy was fantastic for me as it distracted them from the slight tremolo in my nervous voice. Despite my tension, I felt like I belonged here, both as a journalist and as a person. I *wanted* them to notice me. From the moment I met them, I wanted to find a way to be part of their exceedingly cool artistic lives. Their genuine lives. Lives that projected a seeming self-honesty I was striving for.

The interview was fantastic, and they absolutely loved the article I wrote. A week after it ran, I took a chance and invited them to join me as VIP guests at a special Van Gogh exhibition at a local art museum. To my delight, they agreed. I was so shy at the exhibition that I had to write my witty comments about the paintings on a notepad because I couldn't get my voice to not crack. I was desperate to be liked for being me, even if it meant revealing my personal side through bad handwriting.

Both girls were lovely, but I had tunnel vision for Chloe. She had curly dark hair that tumbled down her back in a naturally delicate cascade; soft, dark eyes; an embraceable smile; a brilliant intellect; the sweetest soul and one wickedly irreverent sense of humor. She also had a recently broken heart. A kindred, bruised soul whom I could relate to without stumbling for the words.

The Beastly Ball is one of many exclusive fundraisers held in Los Angeles each year, and it's one of the most delightful. The early summer event is a fundraiser for the Los Angeles Zoo and is held on-site. The top restaurants in the city cater to a VIP crowd clad in designer safari-wear who check out the animals, check out the auction, check out the dance floor, but mostly check out each other. When a press pass to the event crossed my desk inviting me and a guest to the ball, I seized it as my moment to spend some time alone with Chloe and to try to shift her mind from the guy who broke her heart to a guy who wanted to win it.

*

Pasty arms and legs toothpick out from my khaki shorts and shirt as I try my best to look like I belong in the wilds of

Distilling Rob: Manly Lies and Whisky Truths

Africa. Chloe looks like an impossibly lovely jungle heroine who could tame a wildebeest with a blown kiss. I nearly let out a Tarzan-esque yelp when I see her, but I could barely handle the jungle gym in grade school, let alone fly on vines, so I resist the urge.

We board the tram that takes guests from the parking lot to the zoo, as VIPs can't possibly be expected to walk on mere public pavement. Two other people are in our four-person tram compartment, one of them being Stephanie Powers, the stunning redheaded actress of *Hart to Hart* fame, who is engrossed in a cell phone conversation. Before we are even settled into our seats, Chloe jumps all over the celeb encounter situation. She grabs my hand, and my heart jumps all over *that* situation.

"Rob, I just wanted to thank you for the *heart-to-heart* talk we had on the way over here," she says, trying not to laugh.

"The *freeway* was so jammed I figured we had time to chat," I respond in kind, referencing the name of the family dog on *Hart to Hart*.

She bites her lip in order to avoid laughing and takes her hand back to cover her mouth. I already miss her hand.

Throughout the night, we make jokes at the expense of giraffes, stutter over the anatomy of male monkeys, and wonder how quickly the abundance of women in beige leather miniskirts and faux leopard-spot stiletto heels would propel themselves across the African plains if chased by lions. The food is fantastic. The dance floor is festive, and when the music slows, I hold her closely, sway and think, "Wonderful, wonderful, wonderful."

We cross the increasingly thin crowd on the dance floor and return to our table. The ball is winding down, but the time in our little world slows, even as the party's time continues to accelerate to the close. I offer to get Chloe another glass of wine.

"I don't drink much," she smiles, "but, tonight...why not?"

I order a wine for her, pick up a glass of Macallan 18 for myself and return to sit next to her. Before I can raise the whisky to my lips she takes hold of my hand.

"Thank you," she whispers after a moment, and I see tears welling in her eyes. "Tonight has been...perfect. I've had so much fun, and I've forgotten about...you know..."

"Your ex."

"Don't ruin it!" she laughs, releasing my hand.

In a sweeping movement, my hand drops toward the floral arrangement on the table, plucks a tropical flower from the mix and tucks it behind her ear.

"Perfect!" I say as my hand returns to hers, and I mean it. This is a perfect moment. My life and my job uniting with the warm night, the full moon, the excellent whisky, the graceful dancing, the flower in her hair and the light in Chloe's eyes...smile...spirit. Perfect, perfect, perfect, perfect, perfect, perfect...

Our eyes connect. A jet crosses the spotlight of the moon, racing to get its passengers to the other side of the world. Her red lips part slightly, slowly. People move past us fast and with purpose, their time here ended. Her head tilts and the flower's shadow strolls down her perfect neck. Drums thrash in a crescendo as the swing band closes in double time. Her hand tightens its grip. The whisky aroma ascends from the glass to my nose as long-trapped fragrances and spices meet and dance with Chloe's perfume, the tropical flower in her hair and the essence of everything around us. Our bodies, these long-evolved gambles of chromosomes and chance, find ever more proximity to each other. She smiles welcomingly. I lean closer.

Distilling Rob: Manly Lies and Whisky Truths

*

Perfect moments have a time signature all of their own. They linger in their present and last eternally in one's past. The snag lies in the future that follows them.

I didn't try to kiss Chloe that night. I told myself it was out of respect for her healing heart. In truth, I was too fearful to express my feelings. I thought she'd reject me because she would see what I feared deep inside: I wasn't grown-up enough to have a relationship with a woman as wonderful as she.

For the rest of the summer, I held my ever-deepening unrequited feelings to myself. What made it worse is I still was her anchor as she struggled to get over her ex. I listened to her talk about him when all I wanted was for her to hold me. The lonely boy inside me shrank until I felt like I was Atlas holding the weight of the emotional universe on my shoulders.

Finally, in the biggest emotional leap of my life, I told her flat out how I felt. By that point, my hidden turmoil had created so many fissures in our friendship, not to mention my own sanity, that there was no chance for romance. Instead, I cracked into a thousand shards of lunacy.

In case anyone has ever wondered if jumping up on a stage to strip off one's clothes as a belly dancer does her routine in front of a crowd, followed by drunkenly reciting an original love poem in front of said crowd, and, finally, preventing the girl who has rejected your romantic advances from hooking up with the cute guy she's just met – and doing all of this on the most significant birthday night of her life – is the way to win her heart, I tell you firmly, the answer is no. Nor is it a way to retain her friendship.

Chloe had sparked a resurrection of hope within me. Now that she was out of my life, I was shattered. The little boy, who only wanted to be accepted, noticed and loved, was gone. The man he was supposed to transform into had never fully appeared. I was nothing. Amorphous. And I was in the best place in the world to have no self-definition. In Hollywood, if you don't like who you are, you become someone else. So, I did. And he would be nothing like the crying boy I was to abandon.

TWENTY-SIX

MAROONING MYSELF

Friday night. It's like the bell at the end of the school day. The pardon board agreeing that you've served your time. The pastor saying that final "Amen" when the Packers' kickoff is in fifteen minutes. It's about being released.

For some people, Friday night is a release from work. For others, it is a release from routine. Far too many people find it to be a release from themselves: a chance to let go of the tedium of their lives, the misdirection of their hearts and the uncertainty of their existence. Maybe it's all of the above for each of us in one way or another. Whatever it is, Friday night is certainly not like any other night of the week.

Forty hours or so in the last five days have been devoted to moving casks with Aaron and Jack, and occasionally Lewis and Kyle, the warehouse crew supervisors. Supposedly, there is a lot more that goes on in the warehouse than moving casks, such as actually filling them. Every time that task is supposed to be done, an order comes to shift casks within the warehouse or to drive them two miles down the narrow seaside road to the warehouses at Port Charlotte. The filling remains as elusive as the man who is ordering these tasks to be done: Jim

McEwan. Despite my steady progression along the stages of distillery production, I still have not had the chance to sit down with Jim and imbibe his whisky wisdom.

Rain, sleet and snow make the outdoor portions of our cask-moving workweek damn damp. The unheated warehouses make the indoor aspects of our work friggin' frigid. Aaron, Jack and I keep our bodies warm under these circumstances by moving the casks as quickly as possible. We keep our minds from drifting off by sharing life stories, though in the decidedly testosterone-driven way guys do, by focusing on sports, drinking, and women, and sheathing all three in quips, sarcasm and cheekiness.

I've learned that neither guy drinks whisky much at all. What a far cry twenty-first century whisky workers are from their predecessors, who were known to devise dozens of ways to siphon whisky along all avenues of the production and storage process. These boys still like to drink even if it's not whisky. And, tonight, of all nights, is the one to indulge the liver. It's Friday night.

They've invited me to join them for quiz night fun at the Ballygrant Inn pub. I've never been to a quiz night and ask if it involves some kind of computer system or satellite feed. Aaron shakes his head. "We're a little more technologically basic here, but the pencils are indeed sharp."

Ballygrant has at best twenty houses and one inn. The inn is a quarter mile outside of the village, set back along a forest, and is designed like a combination ranch house, diner and community hall. The latter description is most apt, as I have to collect myself when I walk through the well-used door to make sure I'm in the right place. The first people I see are a group of young teenage girls sitting around a table. An eight year-old boy pushes past me as I size up the situation unfolding beneath the bar's bright ceiling lights and he sits down at a table of sixty-year-olds. Four women in their early twenties walk by with too-tight jeans and too-short tops. There's even a large disheveled dog roaming the bar, navigating narrow lanes between tables. This is an Islay menagerie.

I spot Aaron and Jack in the back corner and have to do another double take. The past week, they've been clad in boiler suits, hard hats and grime. Tonight, Aaron is wearing a green t-shirt under a trendy jacket and Jack is sporting the jersey of his favorite football team, the Glasgow Rangers. Both guys are all smiles when they see me. I'd like to think it's because I, too, look cleaned up, but I think it has to do with the pints they're holding and even more to do with the remains of empty pints sitting on the table in front of them.

"Hey!" Jack shouts out. "Here he is, the man who is going to win it all for us. "

"I'll do my best," I declare.

"Aye, you do your best to answer questions, and I'll do my best to get pissed," he laughs.

"Ah, c'mon. You're going to be the anchor for the team!" I encourage him.

"No, he's quite right," Aaron chimes in. "We're fully expecting you to carry the team to victory. We're just going to drink."

Lewis and Kyle couldn't make it, but Abbie, who works in the warehouse office keeping track of the complex cask cataloging system, joins Jack's girlfriend, Emily, as our two female teammates. Abbie is not only sharp enough to handle the quiz challenge, but more importantly, sober enough. Emily is more preoccupied with monitoring the steady flow of beer into Jack than the actual quiz challenge. I don't blame her. At his height, he'll be a massive pain in the ass to lift if his pint consumption inspires him to make a pillow of the floor.

I'm barely settled into my seat before Aaron and Jack each buy me a drink. They feel I won't properly represent the warehouse until the room is adequately blurry. I, on the other hand, am reveling in how the community is coming into focus in a way I haven't seen before. Certainly, I've interacted with my bus-riding crew, chatted with a few shop owners here and there, and spent the workdays with the Bruichladdich team, but this is quite different.

The energy in the pub is almost familial. There are some twenty teams of three to five players each. Middle-aged parents are teamed with their adult kids and their spouses, a couple of younger parents have their preteens with them, groups of retired men and retired women are pitted against each other, there are a handful of workplace teams and a few couples in their twenties out for date night. I'm definitely the odd one in the mix, as everyone knows everyone, and there is pointed yet gentle teasing among the teams as people settle in for the first round.

Our team is tucked away in a corner next to the bar and near the restrooms, so we have a steady stream of people crowding around us. Even as the first set of questions is handed out, people are clamoring for a final round of drinks. I think I see more people at the moment than I've seen in my entire time on Islay, and one blonde girl in particular catches my eye. She looks like Jennifer Lawrence's blonde country cousin and is maybe twelve to fifteen years younger than I. I don't care. It's been a while since I've seen an attractive woman, even if she is only bar-cute. She doesn't notice me, which doesn't bother me. I've been in this position many times before. My dalliances in Hollywood have taught me how to improve the odds that she'll know who I am by the end of the evening. I make a mental note of her and return my focus to the game.

Distilling Rob: Manly Lies and Whisky Truths

Quiz night in Scotland is a throwback, which is appropriate in this setting, as the scope of participants makes me think of this as more of an ancient Celtic ritualistic community gathering than a night out at the pub. The bartender reads questions aloud and teams fill in the blanks on their answer sheets. After each category, sheets are exchanged with a nearby team and answers are checked. I haven't exchanged answer sheets since Father D's history class in high school, and I like this setting better: pints in hand rather than priests looking over your shoulder.

With each passing round, the atmosphere becomes looser. There doesn't seem to be the hyper-attention to competition we have in America and the stress that accompanies it. Or maybe it's the free-flowing alcohol that has people relaxed. Then again, the communal fun could come down to one thing: it's Friday night.

Tonight, I'm all or nothing. I lead the team charge through categories like Hollywood actors and James Bond theme songs. Yes, James Bond theme songs...as though I haven't seen every one of the films fifty times. But, for every *Dr. No* I say yes to, I am shuttered into silence when the category reaches European football, i.e., soccer, teams. My muteness continues with the UK advertising slogan round.

Our team, named by Aaron, is Norfolk and Way (when spoken aloud by the bartender comes across like "No Fuckin' Way") and we're in second place heading into the final round. With each subsequent break between rounds and each subsequent round of drinks between breaks, I eye up the young blonde woman I spotted earlier. While not bad-looking to start with, she gets prettier by the pint. The problem is she isn't looking my way at all.

Final round and we're three points out of first. It's a cryptic clue round about music and there are twelve questions. I know my music. I know my cryptic clues. I don't know why this girl isn't looking at me. I'm getting quite frustrated.

"OK, boys, this is it, so let's pull out this win," says Abbie, who has anchored the team across all categories. "First clue: Gein, Dahmer, Bundy."

"The Killers," I offer, not letting my eyes waver from the blonde.

"Well done!" Jack effuses with sloppy enunciation as he slaps me on the back. He's been the team cheerleader for most of the evening rather than a fount of answers, aside from the football category, which he championed.

Abbie and Aaron pick up the pace on the next several questions. My mind is elsewhere. I don't need a date. I suppose a little companionship would be nice after this much time alone on the island, but at this point all I want is a look. Though I'm certainly older than she, I think I look pretty good tonight, so what is the deal with not even a glance? Wait a second...her eyes are starting to scan the room.

"Deserted quintet?" Aaron muses. "What band is a deserted quintet?"

I tilt my head and steady my gaze. I'm going to give the girl my "look." It's a look I developed during the many, many nights ravaging LA that followed my heartbreak with Chloe. She starts to swivel in this direction.

"Oasis, perhaps?" offers Abbie. "Five members. Oasis is in a desert, which is deserted."

"Aye. So it is!" Jack gushes.

"I'm not quite as certain as you are," Aaron counters.

Distilling Rob: Manly Lies and Whisky Truths

Finally, the girl completes her pivot and her gaze falls on me. I give a little head nod, flick my eyebrows and smile directly at her.

"What do you think, Rob?" Abbie asks.

"Put down Oasis!" Jack insists. "Time is almost up!"

The girl cocks her head, looking slightly confused. I'm in that treacherous ground of having already launched the "look" and not getting the response I'd hoped for. I've never developed a follow-up "look" so I just smile wider. The girl responds with an expression of disregard and turns away.

She? Disregard? Me? Does she have any idea of how many the times the "look" resulted in smiles, phone numbers and discarded lacy things from lovely LA actresses and models? This girl couldn't even get past security to sit in the same bathroom as them, let alone into a Sunset Strip club, and she's disregarding me? I'm the most intriguing option she'll ever have in her entire life on this sea-gripped rock, and I get disregard?

"OK, Oasis it is," concludes Abbie, starting to write down the final answer.

"Maroon Five!" I spit out, now glaring at the back of the girl's head.

"Ah, you could indeed be onto something. Desert, maroon..." Aaron mulls.

"No, no! Oasis! Write it down!" Jack insists.

"It's Maroon Five!" I repeat. Disregard? Me?

"Are you sure?" Abbie asks.

I whip my head away from the girl and back to the table.

"I was onstage singing with them with a blonde all over me who was a hell of a lot hotter than this chick, so fucking write down Maroon Five!"

Our table comes to a confused stop. I look at all the empty beer and whisky glasses in front of me. Whoops. My lubricated lips are more adamant than intended.

"Well then," Aaron finally speaks. "As none of us have, presumably, ever sung onstage with Oasis, I suggest we mark Maroon Five on the answer sheet."

Abbie obliges, and we exchange answer sheets with the next table. Maroon Five is correct, and the rest of our answers move us into final possession of second place. It's victory enough to net the table a couple of bottles of wine and a couple of bottles of whisky. After results are announced Jack asks the question that's been all their minds the past few minutes.

"How the fuck did you get onstage singing with Maroon Five?" Jack asks.

"My friend, anything's possible in Hollywood," I reluctantly say.

"But *you*, onstage..."

"Anything, Jack. For better or worse."

TWENTY-SEVEN

KINGS OF HOLLYWOOD

Friday night. Chad's phone rings. He picks up the slim mobile and looks at the screen in disgust.
"Oh Jesus, not again!" he spits, tossing the phone down to the table and handing the bullshit off to me.

"Is it Macaulay? Is he freaking out because he's home alone and has nothing else to do but bother us?" I volley back with equal derision. I see Chad swallow hard to avoid laughing. He picks up without missing a beat.

"Yeah, now that he's out of rehab, he's such a desperate little fuck," Chad shrugs. "I say we recast with someone whose career I actually give a shit about reviving."

The blonde's big blue eyes grow even bigger. Her face screams Hollywood virgin. So does the face of her twenty-one-year-old brunette friend. Chad and I had been exchanging glances with their too-exposed breasts all evening before saddling up next to them at a bar table. Their clothes are budget attempts at something trendy to make them appear like they belong here in the legendary Chateau Marmont bar on the Sunset Strip. Most of the girls here are in the same situation: young, relatively new to LA and living to be seen at clubs where they will tell anyone who will listen, and many who won't, about their acting class/dialogue coach/unpaid independent film. They tend to forget about the waitress/beer girl/receptionist work they spend most of their time doing, and the knock-off clothes those jobs barely afford them.

Chad and I have preyed upon girls like this for the better part of two years. We met through work after I was shattered by my failure with Chloe and he was ending things with a girl who no longer thrilled him. We treated girls as though they carried for all womankind the original sin of leaving our romantic lives unfulfilled. It's only too easy to dehumanize women who also objectify you solely as the person who can introduce them to the top of the Hollywood food chain and foot the bill to boot.

"Who is Macaulay?" the blonde finally asks in that obvious way that is nowhere near as sly as she thinks it is. Even if it were a slick transition, the way she and the brunette whipped their heads around when Chad said the word, "recast," lets us know that they are interested in one thing. Each duo has entered a chess match of looking for ways to use the other. The distinct advantage lies with the lies Chad and I are so good at spewing.

Chad sighs heavily, making it clear he doesn't want to devote another thought to the matter. He waves at me dismissively, as if to say, "Go ahead, I'm sick of this shit." I roll my eyes and give an agreeing grunt. I slowly lower my head into my hand. The girls lean in. Brilliant.

"Macaulay Culkin," I say. "Remember him, the child actor who's been in and out of rehab lately?"

"Oh my God!" the blonde says in her breathless southern accent. "I totally thought so! When you said, 'home alone,' I was like, 'Oh, my God. Macaulay Culkin?' And it is!"

"Uh, why is he calling both of you guys?" her friend from Iowa says, utilizing all her big words.

"Well..." I start as they lean in even closer. I ease back in my chair. "Nah, that's just boring shit."

"No!" they both squeal. "We want to hear!"

I dramatically drop my head in Chad's direction. He nods nonchalantly for me to continue. The blonde puts her hand on my arm. It's almost easy to the point of being dull.

"We're independent film producers, and we kind of specialize on resurrecting or launching careers," I falsely confess.

The girls drop their jaws like bad actresses. Independent film producers are one of the top "jobs" Chad and I have for this game. Especially with the girls who are new to Hollywood. For women who are a bit beyond their early twenties or who aren't in the film industry, "adult film director" always draws incredible interest, simply because of salacious curiosity. The hands-down best attention getter, far better than the mundane "lawyer," "investment banker," "hedge fund manager" or "music industry agent" is "buyer for Trader Joe's." Seriously. Pulling out that as my "profession" is like fishing with dynamite. Girls love their kale chips and beet salads.

"Yeah," Chad finally sits up. "And this Culkin asshole is clinging to us like a fucking life preserver." On cue, his phone rings again. I glance down to his lap and see him slide his other cell phone back into his pocket. The ol' "fake call," call.

"Is that him again?" the blonde gushes, as she's mesmerized by the actor's name popping up on the phone's display screen.

"Prick," Chad responds, authoritatively not answering the call.

"We've told him...what is it, Chad? Must be ten times..."

"Twenty if anything..."

"...twenty times that we need to cast the two sisters before we know if he's right for the role."

"It's not about you, kid."

"That's right, you told him that."

"I did, and the fucker hasn't stopped calling since."

We grab our drinks on cue and sip our Johnnie Walker Black, single cube, trying to forget pesky Macaulay. The blonde leans to the brunette, and as they rapidly whisper, Chad gives me the look that says he's already bored with them. He taps his watch. It's nearly 1:30 a.m., and we both have to be up to watch college football in the morning.

"It's this or nothing," I mouth. The girls stop whispering and the blonde whips her head back to us.

"Did you say you need to cast two sisters?"

Game. Set. Match. Chad orders a final round of drinks for the table. Now, it's merely a matter of which Casanova gets the blonde and which gets the brunette as we all go to desolation row.

*

Yep. That's me: the child who cowered around strangers, the boy who couldn't talk to girls directly, and the lonely guy who couldn't walk across a bar floor to speak with an equally lonely gal. I'm now a cocky conqueror of beautiful women, wearing expensive couture to complete my character's costume. If I were sixteen and saw that kind of guy in a movie, I would be in awe of his ability to easily meet women and take them home. Now I am one of those characters, unable to share my life and grow gently and truthfully with a partner, so I appropriate female companionship. It's a see and conquer approach to women, devoid of emotional attachment. I am playing the part of my two-dimensional heroes.

Distilling Rob: Manly Lies and Whisky Truths

Chad and I have the perfect backgrounds for these roles. Lost souls launched from childhoods of fear and insecurity. He is as working class as I am, but has already reinvented himself to appear as a cultured and worldly member of the upper echelons of society. I have abandoned the hope of love I had with Chloe and redefined myself with a use 'em and lose 'em attitude toward women matching that of a self-obsessed Hollywood star.

His career in the arts and my Hollywood journalist life give us the stage with which to play our parts. And we feed off each other beautifully, as I adapt myself to his adopted sophistication, and he emboldens his misogynistic attitude toward women with my encouragement, if not example. We are inseparable: two half men who together take Hollywood as one complete LA lothario. And we thrive on that perception night after night, month after month, year after year.

We both know our lives are complete bullshit, and we know the scared place that bullshit comes from: fear of ending up mundane and meaningless. Occasionally, our talks take us to that real place inside where the fear lives and where the hope of ending up better than our dads sometimes shines. The next night, however, we're out again: drinks perpetually in hand, lies perpetually in mouth and wearing an attitude of it doesn't matter if we harm others as long we hide from...we stop before we allow ourselves to think or feel beyond that.

I suppose it would be laudable if I were to end each night out with a sense of shame and regret. But, I don't. There is something amazing and beautiful about the end of a long drunken night of captivating women and pulling all reality into a realm you've created. Sitting with a Scotch in hand at 3:00 a.m. while the rest of LA is fucking, crying or sleeping. Knowing you are alone and more alive in that moment because you've pushed all you are to all you can be to all you think you want to be and have survived the mind fuck you've given yourself. And you've lived for another day.

At least, that's what I told myself. My now-nightly routine of chewing two codeine tablets, washing them down with whisky, and topping it with anti-anxiety meds and sleeping pills tell another story. My emotional heart is all but dead, and it seems I'm trying to kill the beating one as well. There are nights I drift off into blackness with my last thought wondering if I will wake again tomorrow.

The strangest part about this new lifestyle I've created is the deeper and darker I go, the more I encounter the real faces of my fictional heroes. I drink with James Bond (Pierce Brosnan), boldly converse with Captain Kirk (William Shatner), and inundate Indiana Jones (Harrison Ford) with useless personal information. I sleep with actresses whose pretty faces and bodies appear in the films and TV shows I watch. And I party, dance and sing with rock stars, such as, yes, Maroon Five. It's as if I am being rewarded for embracing life in the fast lane by having all my childhood fantasies come true.

In my heart, I know that the younger me – the boy who had hoped for meaningful love, who dreamed that one day he could grow into the kind of man that could make a positive difference in the world – would be disgusted by, and even worse, ashamed of the person I've become. And I scoff at that thought. That younger me struggled day in and day out to be comfortable in his own skin. Now I am living a life that men around the world fantasize about having. Me. Little Robby Gard from Beloit, Wisconsin. The younger me could go to hell, for all I care.

I refuse to acknowledge that the "me" I've constructed is well on his way there.

TWENTY-EIGHT

MANNING UP

I'm mortified as I make the Monday morning walk to the warehouse at a turtle's pace. Earlier I wished in vain that my bed comforter could be a shell to hide me so I wouldn't have to face life today. Friday night ended awkwardly after my drunken outburst at the pub quiz. The warehouse crew and I went our separate ways at the end of the evening with hardly an additional word spoken.

Saturday only added to this morning's short and slow steps up the frost-covered path to the warehouse. That afternoon, I'd run into Bruichladdich's managing director while on a stroll. Since my first day working at the distillery, I'd blogged about my experiences and added photos as needed. Friday's blog featured my thoughts about the warehouse and included a picture of Aaron standing atop a pile of empty casks rearranging them. The Managing Director urgently stopped me as we walked near each other and firmly requested that I remove that photo from my blog. Aaron, it turns out, isn't supposed to stand on loosely arranged piles of casks. Not wearing a hard hat only made the photo worse, and he is concerned that the image could reach the eyes of safety inspectors. I assure him that I will remove it immediately, and I do. But, that doesn't leave me reassured as I reach the gigantic warehouse door on this icy morning. I worry that word of his displeasure has reached Aaron, Jack and everyone else I'm supposed to work with all week long.

The wooden sliding door runs almost the entire height and length of the front part of the warehouse. When fully opened, trucks can drive through it. I'm trying to sneak in without drawing too much attention, but there is no way to move something that massive and be subtle about it. To make matters worse, as soon as I crack the door a few inches I see that today is the day we will finally be filling empty casks instead of spending eight hours moving full ones. The filling area is thirty feet from the door. Aaron and Jack stand along a row of empty casks. Both turn toward me slightly as the door creaks open further. They immediately turn away.

I lug the door closed behind me and venture another cautious look toward the guys. A row of casks sits above a trough on the warehouse-floor side of a cement retaining wall. On the other side of the wall, pipes run from steel holding tanks to a filling station where a pump feeds whisky into a gas hose and nozzle. Jack walks from cask to cask, placing barcoded labels on individual barrels that will track their content and movement for the next ten to thirty years. Aaron rolls an empty cask so that a small opening on its side is facing up for filling. He walks to the hose and starts to fill the cask. I turn away and enter the warehouse office to retrieve my hard hat and to find out what I'm doing for the day.

Abbie and the two warehouse managers, Kyle and Lewis, sit in the office. All three look up as I enter and quickly return to their work before making eye contact with me. I hesitantly pick up my hard hat.

Distilling Rob: Manly Lies and Whisky Truths

"Am I going to be helping Aaron and Jack again today?" I haltingly ask.

Kyle, who has a Bruce Willis look about him, peers up momentarily and gives me a stare that has me worried he's going to say, "Yippee-ki-yay, motherfucker," and kick my ass on the spot for photographing a safety violation on his watch. He gives a half nod in the direction of the door. I'm not sure if this means, "Yes," or if it means, "We welcomed you into our warehouse brotherhood and then you betray our trust by putting up a picture for the entire world to see that makes us look like reckless idiots." Then again, that interpretation could be rooted more in my guilt than in his glance. I walk out and head toward Aaron and Jack.

I pray there isn't a mention of my Maroon Five bombast. I didn't come here to shine a spotlight on my past. I just want to be one of the guys, working in the darkness of the warehouse without unwanted attention. And now, I've given *them* unwanted attention with my photo post.

"Morning, boys," I shake out of my throat as I approach. Aaron eases off the pump and Jack stops labeling. Neither offers an immediate response to my weak greeting. Less than seventy-two hours ago, they were two of my only friends on the island. At the moment, I feel they view me as their biggest enemy.

Jack takes his gloves off and tosses them on top of a cask. He steps forward, grinding the knuckles of his right hand into his left palm. All 6 feet 7 of him comes to an abrupt stop less than a foot from me. I tilt my head up to meet his eyes. Suddenly, his arms fly wide. I flinch and try to step back. He throws his arms around me.

"Here he is! The hero who led us to second place!" he proclaims as he holds me in a playful hug.

"Without your cerebral prowess, we certainly wouldn't have been able to get away with drinking as much as we did," Aaron laughingly chimes.

"Saturday morning was a fucking waste. My head still fucking hurts," Jack admits as he releases me.

"Well that may have as much to do with Saturday night's drinking as with Friday's quiz," Aaron deduces.

"I was drinking Saturday to get rid of the fucking pounding in my head from Friday."

"And what is your excuse for last night?"

"I was just getting pissed to get pissed."

They laugh and I feel absolved and released from the fear that strangled me all weekend. It's time to get to work.

Once the new spirit arrives here from the still house for casking, it is stored in one of three sterile stainless steel tanks that coldly glow under pale florescent lights. The large tanks are slightly separated from the cask area by that low cement wall. The effect is one of alienation: these unattractive tanks that don't hold the whisky for any appreciable length of time aren't worthy of being on the same plane as the wizened and well-traveled casks.

Truth be told, the empty casks aren't particularly striking either. They have much more mythical appeal when they're filled, racked and gently influencing the whisky as it ages. We arrange sixty of them in an organized fashion for labeled cataloging. They're battered, worn and dirty. Old soldiers that aren't much to look at, but you'd want them on your side to see you through the rough times.

I fill each cask as Aaron monitors the flow on an LCD screen. Our job is to fill the casks as close to capacity as possible without overflowing, and record how much liquid is poured into each cask. The trough catches any spilled whisky, but that is discarded. The goal is to not leak any into the trough. With all the time and effort that's gone into making the whisky at this point (not to mention all of Budgie's stories this liquid had to bear), the last thing we want is to lose the new-make spirit.

"Do you guys ever stop to think about the whisky? This stuff you're making right here on Islay is going to end up on the other side of the world," I muse as I start filling another cask.

"Aye, it's pretty cool," Jack says. "People in all these other countries know about Islay all because of the whisky."

"The economic impact of the island's distilleries is pretty substantial," Aaron adds. "We very well may be one of the most famous islands in the world."

"Well, I don't know about that. We don't have a hell of a lot of bikinis on the beach," Jack drawls.

"Very true. We are perhaps the most famous island in the world without the benefit of mostly nude women," Aaron corrects himself.

"How does that make you feel, though? You guys do all this work, spend years, decades, maturing the whisky, and then most of it is sent away," I inquire as I raise a battered mallet to pound a cork into another filled cask.

"I have a job out of it, is what I think," Jack says.

"And really, if we had to drink all of it here at the distillery, I think we'd struggle to get anything done during the day," Aaron adds.

"Aye, we'd just be pissed all the time," Jack says.

"Actually, that doesn't sound too bad, does it?" Aaron responds

"No it doesn't. Except I'd rather be pissed on lager than whisky," Jack says.

"You already are pissed on lager most of the time," Aaron jokes.

"Aye, but I don't get paid for it."

We share a big laugh as I finish off the latest cask. With the nozzle in my hand, I feel like a gun-slinging cowboy calmly making sure my client finds its way to the cask stagecoach so it can reach its full potential.

"I've been thinking," Jack says. "Hollywood is kind of like Islay."

"How so?" I ask and pause the filling.

"Yes, please do share this insight," Aaron says.

"You make movies there and the rest of the world watches them," he offers.

"True, but we get to keep the movie stars."

"Aye, there you go."

"And, of course, you get to sing on stage with the rock bands as well," Aaron points out, dashing any hope that my drunken boast was overlooked.

"Yeah, I forgot about that," says Jack as he pauses from labeling casks. "Have you met many famous people?"

I hesitate. The answer is yes, to the extreme. There are few famous Hollywood faces I haven't met through interviews or at parties and fundraisers. It all seems like another life to me now, and my relationship with that fantasyland on the other side of the world seems as permanently distant as the dream of marrying Katie. My head screams at me to not answer the question. I want to be one of the guys, not some elitist from Hollywood. After a few breaths, I decided to ignore my head. I need to be honest with these two friends.

"Yes, I have," I finally answer.

"Who?" Jack blurts out the question I'd expected, but hoped to avoid.

"Well, if you name someone, I probably met them or was at an event with them. I was a newspaper editor in Hollywood, so I came across a lot of famous people," I respond, trying to deflect the subject.

"Does anyone in particular stand out?" Adam asks as he walks closer.

"Aye, what are they like in person?" Jack, too, is closing in out of curiosity.

I stand up from the cask I am filling and lower my nozzle sidearm.

"To be honest, most of the people I met are nothing like what you see on the screen." They both listen keenly. "Sometimes they're shorter, their skin isn't as great as it is on screen, they aren't as sophisticated, charming or intelligent as you'd imagine. Some are goofy, some are gentle, some are cocky, some are extremely nice and kind, some are bastards."

"They're no different from anyone else," Jack interrupts.

I nod.

"Are there any who aren't so ordinary? Any who really stand out as being larger than life?" Aaron asks.

I don't even have to consider this question, as the answer is often at the front of my mind.

"Clint Eastwood," I quickly reply.

"Any particular reason why?" inquires Aaron.

I shrug nonchalantly.

"He just is," I lie.

In truth, Clint Eastwood may have saved my life.

TWENTY-NINE

BY NECESSITY, NOT DESIGN

When I was ten, I jumped on my bike and rode it through our neighborhood on a warm and windy summer day. Still feeling energetic, I rode it a few blocks further from familiar homes to areas that were recognizable, but definitely not my neighborhood. Those few blocks expanded to a mile and a half, where I reached my grade school playground, empty for the summer. There I lingered, briefly, thinking about a return home. The thought didn't remain long, and neither did I. Instead, I pedaled onward, crossing the bridge over the Rock River to the other side of town. I huffed my Huffy all the way to Beloit's only mall, which stood atop a very steep hill (for a ten-year-old) overlooking the river and the industrial steam rising over the west side of town. There, I stopped with the exhaustion of sweat and thirst. I was tired, far from home and dreading the distance I needed to pedal to return. I started to panic, which must have been evident to people walking in and out of the Sears store where I sat slumped against a wall.

A stranger lent me money for a pay phone, and I called my mom, crying about my predicament, begging her to rescue me.

Instead of the sympathy I'd expected, I was greeted with outrage that I'd taken off on such an ill-advised journey. Mom refused to get in the car to retrieve my bike and me, saying I had gotten myself there, it was up to me to get myself back, and hung up in anger. I had no options. No safety net. I rode, walked and pushed that bike the endless six miles back to the house. It was the hardest thing I'd ever done in my life. When I finally made it home, I dramatically collapsed in the front entryway, at Mom's feet, to make her feel guilty. It didn't work.

"Sometimes, Robby, you just have to do things on your own," she said firmly, "especially when you create your own mess."

*

That's where I was with my life in LA: at the metaphorical phone booth, begging for someone to pick me up because I didn't have the energy to take myself to a place of safety. Everything was a blur. I didn't recognize where I was and had no idea how to retrace my steps to return to someplace familiar. My life was night after night of partying and philandering broken up by robotic workdays. I had enough skill and experience as a journalist to get the job done and to do it well, but there was no passion behind it. I used the job to give me access to those endless Hollywood nights.

I don't know why, but somewhere in the midst of that crazy living I decided to start a relationship with a woman. Maybe she was like the stranger who gave me money to call my mom. I needed some kind of help and she was there.

Shawnie was an interior designer who lived in Orange County, which was forty miles from my apartment and a million miles from Hollywood. I still went out with Chad a few nights each week, and we were as decadent as ever, but when I went down to Shawnie's on weekends I found a safe house.

In some ways, Shawnie reminded me of Chloe. The curly dark hair, warm smile and kind heart. But, she was very different in other ways. Where Chloe was a challenge to my intellect and a saber to my wit, Shawnee was more like the 1950s girl next door – sweet, straightforward, and easygoing. Chloe dreamed of being on the stages of the world, singing the most complex arias ever composed. Shawnee dreamed of being at home, singing simple lullabies to her future children.

My need at the time was probably not much more complex than that of a child. I needed shelter, comfort and love. She gave that to me, without hesitation. I couldn't emotionally connect with her, but she either didn't see that or refused to believe it. In some ways, I played "boyfriend" with her the same way I played "movie producer" with the one-night flings. I didn't do it because I wanted to deceive her or lead her on; I simply wasn't capable of anything more. I needed a retreat from the insanity and she gave it to me.

One night as I clumsily kissed her, she sarcastically said that her goal in life was to be close to me at least once when I didn't smell like alcohol. I joked that I couldn't help it; all the delicious desserts she regularly baked for me called for whisky accompaniment. Her comment and my response left both of us feeling distant the rest of the night.

The next day, I couldn't get what she said out of my mind. She was right. Throughout my entire adult life I rarely came near a woman without first having a drink, and by a drink I mean several. Even with Shawnie, whom I'd been dating for several months, I always had at least a couple of whiskies before we ended up in her bedroom.

I'm not sure if I was trying to prove a point to myself or if I was simply curious as to what would happen, but I decided to stop drinking when I was around Shawnie. The decision took no physical effort to implement. As much as I liked a good drink, followed by a few more, I never had a problem with alcohol in terms of an addiction. I sometimes didn't touch a drop for weeks at a time because I didn't feel like it. But, this time, there was a challenge I couldn't anticipate.

Shawnee was thrilled when I told her I was taking a break from drinking around her. She took it as a sign of commitment to her and to the ring, house and family that would inevitably follow such a loving, giving act. However, her excitement and my entire mental balance were quickly dashed, and it had nothing to do with the drinking resolution. Almost immediately after I gave up drinking around her, whenever she'd reach for me, even for a hug, I'd respond with a recoiling cringe. The response came automatically, without thought or warning.

Shawnie pleaded with me to tell her what was wrong, why I no longer wanted to hold her, let alone make love to her, and I couldn't give her an answer. I didn't know if I was over her and the whole relationship, or if the schizophrenic nature of my life – Hollywood partying and Orange County suburbia – had finally stretched me apart.

I felt my mind crumbling. I told Shawnie I needed a few days break, which sent her into a meltdown. Chad asked me to stay home instead of going out because I was too depressing to be around, which didn't make for a good wingman. Sleep was shattered every night with me waking in a panic, like something was clawing through a partially opened door, and I was unable to open it to let it in or close it to keep it out. Work was miserable, as I couldn't concentrate on writing articles, editing my reporters' work or even the relatively mind-numbing task of designing the paper.

As much as I wanted to crawl in a cave somewhere and figure out what was wrong with me, I still had a job to do.

Distilling Rob: Manly Lies and Whisky Truths

*

Celebrity photographers project an image of sleazy guys who are one step above, if not in step with, criminal activity. Scruffy, unwashed, snarling, ready to pick a fight at any moment. I suppose many of the pursuit paparazzi might fit this description. The celebrity photographers who surround me at the moment are nothing like that. They're more like the people you'd expect to read *People*, the *National Enquirer* and *Entertainment Weekly* than the professionals who provide the photos.

Janice, dressed in Walmart overstock, is in her late forties and is bulky enough to take up space for two photographers; Bob is grandfatherly in a tobacco-tinged-fingers, bingo-playing kind of way; James looks like he should be running an overly warm college bookstore instead of standing outside on this cold night; and the green and pink-haired Amy should be in community college, working nights as a waitress and buying books from James. Another dozen photographers I know from the celebrity circuit are also crowded with us beneath the spotlights sweeping the Hollywood sky. Though I run a small local newspaper, I have a special position in the front and center of these competitive photogs, as I am also a writer and need to have access to celebrities to ask questions. That makes the rest of the camera-wielding group, most of whom sell their pictures to worldwide publications, hate me.

We stand outside on a January night in front of Hollywood's historic Egyptian Theatre, impatiently waiting for our target. For the past hour, we've watched trendsetters, hipsters and starlets stream down the red carpet past rows of twinkle-light-wrapped palm trees and into the theatre for a special screening of *Mystic River*. Some of the photographers take polite photos to make the B- and C-listers feel like they're important, but Janice repeatedly shoots down any rising egos with loud exclamations of, "They're nobody!" This screening isn't for celebrities in as much as it's for film buffs. The film was nominated for several Academy Awards a few days ago, and tonight director Clint Eastwood is going to hold a question-and-answer session after the screening.

Clint Eastwood. The name resonates like a sledgehammer on stone. Of all my childhood heroes, the icons of manhood, Clint always loomed largest. James Bond, Indiana Jones, Captain Kirk – they were incredible men in extraordinary, but quite fictional settings. Clint, on the other hand, played a man's man in his films. A guy you'd expect to find on the Western frontier, the mean city streets or charging across a battlefield. At the same time, he'd exude a vulnerability and compassion few other tough guy actors could in movies like *Honkytonk Man*, *Bronco Billy* and *Bridges of Madison County*. In my mind, from the time I was a child to this very moment waiting for his arrival, Clint was everything a man could be whether he had a gun in his hand or a tear in his eye.

My phone vibrates in my pocket for the fifth time in the last hour. It's probably Shawnie again, wondering why I haven't even emailed her today. She's desperate for some attention, some reassurance that this is a break and not a breakup. I can't give her that answer. I can't give myself answers to my behavior because I'm still not sure of the questions. Even here, under the distracting glare of camera lights and sequined dresses, my distress consumes me.

Rumbles, roars and claps help me focus on the moment. Clint's limo has arrived. The melee in the photo pit starts, as elbows and hips work to make space for the perfect picture. Twenty cameras aiming from the same angle looking for a unique shot.

Distilling Rob: Manly Lies and Whisky Truths

Clint steps out and the crowd erupts. Bystanders and autograph seekers, cordoned off from the main walkway by a rope and security guards, haphazardly aim pocket cameras and thrust pens and paper at the movie star. He politely waves and smiles, continuing down the red carpet without pause.

There's a media hierarchy for red carpets, with photographers first, writers second and television last so they can spend the longest time with the stars. My role as a writer and photographer makes me one of the first people to talk to Clint. Despite hundreds of celebrity interviews and interactions, I still get nervous. In my fragile state of mind, and with all Clint means to me, I'm woozy by the time he stops just two feet away. His seriously focused media handler hastily points at me, and I'm on for my one question, face-to-face with the manliest man this boy ever wanted to be.

"Mr. Eastwood, what inspired you to direct *Mystic River*?" I quickly blurt.

He pauses and nods at me. Thank God I asked a good question. And it's a question that he's probably answered five hundred times by this point, so he has his response at the ready.

"I've always been fascinated with the stealing of innocence," he replies slowly and clearly as I scribble away. The man knows how to work with the media, yet another tick of the box of what makes him such an icon. "Crimes against children are heinous and certainly a capital crime if ever there was one. That's what attracted me to this story – the fact that something monstrous that happened in childhood is still alive in adulthood."

He smiles and is gone. I finish scribbling down his quote – "monstrous...happened in childhood...alive in adulthood."

"Hey!" yells Janice, giving me a thick elbow to the ribs. "Watch where the hell you're going!"

I apologize for stumbling into her and step away, only to bump into another photographer who also growls at me for messing up his shot. Standing in one place is not easy at the moment. I feel weak, my heart is racing, the crowd noise thickly crawls into my ears, and my legs struggle to support me. Somehow, I slide beneath the boundary rope without falling and straggle down the red carpet, away from all the action. A couple of security people say things, but I can't hear them. I need to leave.

Now.

I'm on my living room couch, hazy about how I arrived here with only vague recollections of finding my car and driving through Hollywood. No thoughts seem to cross my mind. I'm catatonically crushed beneath the weight of something I can't see. I flash back to Clint. He doesn't seem real. Words come to me and I hear his tough and compassionate voice: "Something monstrous that happened in childhood is still alive in adulthood..."

I curl up so tightly I can't get any smaller.

THIRTY

UNFORGIVEN

My thirteen-year-old Uncle Dan lies on the upper part of his unkempt bunk bed. The bed below is piled high with clothes and trash. The trash may be cleaner than the clothes. He holds a Black Sabbath album sleeve in his hand, his stoned eyes dully looking over the album photos, if they're doing anything at all. Dark grinding guitars and the wicked wail of a voice stretch through the tiny speakers of his stereo in stark contrast to the bright summer afternoon. The room reeks of stale cigarette smoke carried in from my grandparents' living room, on the other side of his bedroom door.

Distantly, through the closed door, I hear my mom chattering to her parents while my grandpa yells at the TV. The Cubs must be losing, again. As much as I love baseball, even though I'm five, I am eager to leave the adult chatter and the seventh-inning stretch on the other side of the door. There's a far more exciting adventure to be found in here,

I've come into Dan's room to play with his ignored G.I. Joes. Ozzy and weed now occupy my uncle's free time the way these toys must have once kept him busy for hours on end. I'm oblivious to his current pursuits. I mean, I'm five. But these

G.I. Joes are sources of endless fascination: the steely stares, chiseled muscles, uniforms and guns. There's no other toy like them. These plastic men are much smaller than me, but they stand large in my world. At preschool, I often sit alone in a corner and pretend I am a G.I. Joe, shooting at the other kids who have kidnapped my friend Joey from me.

Dan and I aren't alone in his room. His friend John is there as well. Friend may be a loose definition. They hang out, apparently with the wary eyes of law enforcement on them when they roam the streets of Beloit. I often hear adults whisper the term, "reform school," indicating where these two will be sent if trouble continues. Both Dan and John have the early puberty equivalents of beards and long, greasy hair that excretes the musty aroma of marijuana. I feel so undersized around them. Dan has always been a bit strange, but lets me play with his toys. John, on the other hand, scares me.

John is at Dan's long desk, sitting on a wobbly rolling chair near the door. He stabs modeling clay with a putty knife in rhythm with the pounding music and watches me play with the G.I. Joes as they go on the attack. I muffle the war sounds as much as possible the more his stare crawls over me.

"You're such a little pussy," he says in a frighteningly flat tone. I ignore him. His tone quickly changes. "Hey, Robby! I said you're a little pussy! You would never shoot anyone because you're such a pussy."

I look to my uncle who hasn't moved his eyes from the album cover. I put my focus back on the G.I. Joes. One of them drops a gun. I tremble as I try to put it back in his hands. "Come here," John growls. Again, I ignore him as I fumble with the gun, unable to control my shaking. "I said come here, you little pussy!"

Distilling Rob: Manly Lies and Whisky Truths

His scornful tone makes my heart race and again I look to my uncle. Dan pays no attention, as he's pulled out the lyrics sheet and is trying hard to focus on reading it. I reluctantly make eye contact with John who points at me with the putty knife and motions for me to come over. I'm five. He's thirteen. I do what I'm told.

Submissively, I put the men down, leaving the tough guys and their guns behind me. I have no protection. I walk to John with as much enthusiasm as I have when I see my dad take his belt off and order me to lie across his knees. I stumble to a stop in front of John who smiles with a malevolence befitting the music pulsating around us.

"Take your pants off, pussy," he demands. I feel my eyes, my entire face, open wide. I urgently look to Dan who still pays no attention. John grabs my head and forces it back his direction. "Take your fucking pants off."

He laughs as my hands shake uncontrollably. He gives my hair a yank as I fumble to undo my belt and zipper. I drop the pants to my ankles and stand in front of him in just my underwear.

"Man, you are a pussy. Is your dick really that small? Do you even have a dick?" he breathes as he slowly inches the chair closer to me. He points the putty knife at me with his right hand. His left hand creeps toward me and he slowly slides it inside my underwear. His skin feels filthy and rough. I am motionless. His awful fingers reach around my testicles until they rest in his palm. His gaze is unyielding, as is his emotionless smile.

Slowly, at first, he flexes his fingers until they press my testicles firmly against his hand. His grip grows tighter. I feel my breath catch and my legs weaken. His smile seems more fulfilled. Without warning, he fully squeezes me as hard as he can.

"What are you going to do, pussy?" he asks, his voice in a sudden whisper. "Are you going to be a pussy and yell for your mommy? She's right out there." He nods to the closed door. "Are you going to cry for mommy, tough guy?"

I look to the door with such intensity that it should splinter, but I don't speak. All I need to do is yell for Mommy to come save me. I just want Mommy. Why can't Mommy be here? What is Mommy doing? What can't she help me? Please open the door, Mommy! Please. Mommy...

I remain silent. John laughs and twists his grip.

"Like I told you, you're a little pussy."

Tears drip down my face. Tears of pain, tears of helplessness, tears of naked shame.

"Pussy."

I still can't bring myself to call out for Mommy. How can she abandon me like this?

"John, stop it." The voice belongs to my uncle and it sounds more annoyed than avenging. John squeezes so tight that all breath drains from me.

"John, stop!" my uncle says again.

John lets go. But, I don't feel released.

*

I whimper and shake as I look around my LA living room, still prone on the couch. I go over the incident with John and my uncle again. And again. And again. Each time, details become clearer, like an image appearing as grime is scraped away from a long-forgotten mural. I struggle to understand. I don't believe in any repressed memory bullshit. Don't those stories come from people who are weak, disturbed, looking to find any excuse to explain their fucked up lives? That's not me. Is it?

"Something monstrous that happened in childhood is still alive in adulthood," Clint's voice is clear again.

I think about shrinking back from Shawnie's touch, the years of drunken sex that numbed me to my naked vulnerability, the inability to connect with women, the struggles to stand as an equal to other men and the trembling around authority figures. I think about every damn problem I've ever had. Things I've done, embarrassments unleashed, fears exposed. Decades of actions and reactions fly at me under the light of this new "memory." I hate it. I hate IT. I want to kill this thing. But, it doesn't go away. It repeats and pounds and punishes.

I feel smaller and smaller. I feel a lifetime slipping away as this memory becomes more and more real. I'm overwhelmed that my entire life has been a lie and all my actions have been built upon a horrible experience that I've blocked from my mind. I feel robbed. Deeply and wholly robbed of whatever essence I thought was me. I cry harder at the thought. I ache beyond words, knowing all I had to do was call out for Mommy. I hurt even deeper knowing all she had to do was open the door. Why couldn't she protect me? Why *didn't* she protect me? Aren't parents supposed to be all-knowing and all-seeing? But, there was no way for her to know or to see.

"Crimes against children are heinous," I hear Clint say and I am momentarily pulled out of the endless pit this memory has opened up. I say a silent prayer of thanks to Clint. Finally, one of my fictional heroes has come through in real life and shined a spotlight on the demons that had lurked invisibly around me. But, I fear it's too late. I'm too far down the path of wrong decisions and evaporated opportunities for any sort of life redemption. I don't know where I'd even begin or if any part of me is even capable of going a new direction.

Who and what am I?

THIRTY-ONE

ECHOES OF IMPRESSIONS

Arguments are fierce in the whisky community over where the essence of the spirit comes from. Is it the grain? Does fermentation play the biggest role? The shape of the stills affecting how the alcohol is collected? The cask types? The warehouse environment? Where does this thing we call whisky come from? For whatever reason, people feel the need to pinpoint the fundamental nature of whisky.

"It's a drink. You drink it. That's what you do," Matty says succinctly, summarizing his thoughts on the matter as we have a wee blather at the Lochindaal.

"I agree," I reiterate for the third time in our conversation. "But some people want to pinpoint the exact moment of impact where a whisky's future is determined. They want to say, 'Aha! *This* is why the whisky tastes like apple cinnamon crisps on a warm fall day after a light rain.'"

Matty nods as he takes another swig of Budweiser. The Lochindaal is hopping at the moment. Aaron and Jack are watching a soccer game on the telly along with a couple of other guys. Two elementary schoolers and a very drunk forty-year-old are playing billiards. Johnny Cash sings low from the jukebox about a boy named Sue.

"Aye," Matty finally says. "Thing is, Robby, you can run yourself mad looking for the answer, and right when you think you have it, the fucking bottle drops and shatters, and you have nothing for it."

I'm about to respond when the understated bar din is pierced by a shriek. One of the young boys sprints to the bar from the billiards table, his face bright red and tears flying. The people watching the soccer game turn around as I do, and the older of the two men with Jack and Aaron leaps from his barstool toward the boy.

"Dad! He kicked me! He kicked my hand!" the boy trembles through his tears, pointing at the forty-year-old man, who is hot on the kid's heels.

"I'm sorry, Logan, I'm sorry!" the man shouts to the dad. "Your lad kept moving the pool balls around and I..."

"Why the fuck did you kick me boy!"

"I told you..."

By now the boy has reached his dad, who no longer pays attention to his crying son. He pushes the boy backwards as he lunges for the drunken kicker. The boy is trapped between the two and looks at his dad in terror.

"No, Dad, no!"

The boy's words are ignored as his dad lands an overhand hook against the left eye of his son's attacker. Dad shoves the boy out of the way and grabs the pool player by the collar, swinging away as he drives him out the backdoor and into the alley. Matty hasn't moved; his eyes are fixed on the door as he takes another swig of beer. Jack turns his attention to the boy, whose hand is quickly swelling.

"Let's see it," he says.

"It's broken! He broke my hand!" The boy is in hysterics.

"It's not broken, but you need some ice on there," advises Aaron, after he, too, examines the boy.

The kid doesn't respond. He cries unabashedly, eyes fixed on the door where his dad disappeared. I can see through those tears a kind of awareness that grows the longer his dad is away. This kid knows that whatever is happening out there started because he kept messing with the pool table during the game. I sense he's crying for his dad being in a fight as much as he's crying over his swollen hand.

As I watch this kid tremble and stare searchingly at the door I can't help speculate how these few minutes, which started with his being nothing more than a bratty little boy, may hound and haunt his heart and mind for the rest of his life.

Maybe it doesn't matter which influences impact the taste of whisky most when it is finally imbibed. All that matters is that it somehow comes out right in the end.

THIRTY-TWO

AND SO IT GOES

Smack!

The echo of the punch bounces its way from the back of the bus all the way to the driver, whose eyes shoot up to the rearview mirror to scan the vehicle for the source of the sound.

I have just hit Moody Smith's nose with every ounce of strength my eleven-year-old fist possesses. We are public enemies number one and two in our school, but this is our first confrontation. Most of the time, we come across each other in the principal's office, each of us there for a different offense. I am the disruptive brat of our small Lutheran school. He is the hulking brute. Moody is a grade ahead of me, fifty pounds heavier than me, and a hell of a lot meaner than me.

He also has my candy bar in his hand at this very moment.

Earlier that day, I had been given the candy bar in honor of my birthday, though my birthday is months away. The school's policy is to give birthday boys and girls a candy bar at lunchtime and have everyone sing to make them feel special. To make those of us with summer birthdays feel included, we are feted with the same enthusiasm three months before our actual birthdays. Candy bar day is something I've looked forward to all school year. Now that my awesome day is here, Moody Smith tries to take it away from me on the bus ride home.

At this point, the candy bar is moot. Between his grabbing for it and my struggle to hang on to my precious, whatever remains in the wrapper is a melted mash. I no longer want the candy bar. I want justice.

With that comes the unbridled punch.

The sound of the smack dissipates, replaced by the sharp intake of breath coming from dozens of schoolchildren who have improbably witnessed the puny punk hit the big bully. Everything stops.

Time creeps back into motion as a smile slowly edges out along Moody's lips. His nose, which still bears the redness of my punch, twitches once and then again. His smile broadens and seemingly pulls his right arm back as the grin spreads along his face.

Snap!

I don't even remember seeing his fist fly at me. All I know is that somewhere between the start of his sadistic smile and the bus pulling over, my nose has been broken and what seems like half my blood is splattered all over the seat and my shirt. Moody reaches his other hand to me.

"You can have your stupid candy bar," he says, thrusting it in my face.

"Keep it," I gurgle as I swoon back.

*

Memories like this have flooded me the past few weeks. Incidents I recall clearly but haven't dusted off in some time have come in waves since the memory of the incident in my uncle's room surfaced. Each story that I recall is about me standing up to bullying, whether by a violent preteen when I was a kid or by a verbally aggressive boss as an adult.

Years of my life felt robbed and raped the night Clint triggered my memory. I was thrown back to a defenseless five-year-old on the inside. I spent what seemed like every conscious moment and restless dream state reviewing my life through the prison of what my uncle's friend had done to me. At first I felt like everything I had done in my life was fraudulent. This incident was so powerful that I'd blocked it, and to me, that meant whatever course my life was supposed to have taken before that incident was also blocked from ever coming to fruition. And, of course, the life that didn't happen was free of the insecurities and shortcomings of the life I ended up having.

I shared my struggles with my best friend Mike, who was serving with the Army in Iraq. Through a series of emails he reassured me that there is no way a single incident can dictate every moment of the rest of our lives. We are the sum of our parts.

Thanks to his advice and support, I made several key decisions to help me move forward. Things with Shawnie came to a crashing end, but one that was ultimately good for both of us. She deserved better than someone using her as a crutch and abusing the love she wanted to share. My endless nights of delicious depravity on the Hollywood scene with Chad were also drastically curtailed. I stopped my nightcaps of prescription meds and cocktails.

These changes were like getting hold of a map into myself. Or maybe pulling a map out of myself. Perhaps a little bit of both. The end result was that I could see how that childhood incident led me down some dark paths in my life. However, the experience also gave me an internal strength to stand up for myself and to fight for what I thought was right throughout my life. I was too scared to run out of my uncle's bedroom door to escape the clutches of a disturbed young man. But maybe what I was unable to do when I was five gave me the strength to walk out of my parents' door for a bold move to Colorado when I was seventeen, and later out of my own front door for an even riskier move to LA.

One day in my uncle's bedroom forever altered my childhood and kept me chained to a path not of my choosing. Remembering that day as an adult would free me to take a new direction.

THIRTY-THREE

WHISKY VOWS

Flowers are everywhere at the distillery today. Mary, who runs the gift shop, has raided the gardens of homes near Bruichladdich and ripped away every yellow tulip she could find. The native Ileach is the consummate ambassador for the distillery and the island, as she was formerly the director of the local history museum before being brought on board by Bruichladdich to welcome visitors from around the world. At the moment, Mary the emissary is little more than a common vandalizing thief. Her plucked plunders are all gathered with the most noble of purposes though: today there is a wedding at Bruichladdich.

Duncan has pulled me away from the warehouse and left Aaron and Jack to handle the workload alone. My job today is helping Mary bring loads of whisky-filled glasses from the gift shop to the still house for a post-"I Do" toast. I'm not thrilled about this change of work tasks. I feel an intense devotion to the warehouse team, and I don't want to let them down by not being there to give the guys a hand. However, deep down, I know my unhappiness with the wedding assignment has little to do with the warehouse. This will be the first wedding I've been to in more than four years. I had once hoped the wedding drought would have been satiated by my own nuptials to Katie sometime in that span. I've avoided weddings ever since that hope died.

My conflicted feelings are hidden as the wedding preparation activity increases.

The still house's boiling stills and hot pipes are accented by ribbons of tartan featuring "Bruichladdich Blue," which matches the color of the sea loch that borders the distillery. Pots of white daisies surround the still bases, and two casks stand between the spirit safes, each crowned with a loose collection of lilies. The pilfered tulips are strategically placed throughout the distillery courtyard and in the gift shop.

Compared to the normal distillery décor of scattered tools, brooms and misplaced hard hats, Bruichladdich looks practically posh. All the effort is for good reason as a German couple and their friends descend upon the distillery for a midweek afternoon wedding. Hans and Eva are fans of Bruichladdich and certainly don't mind each other, so they have chosen the distillery as the place to tie their lifelong knot. The setting is appropriate. There are a thousand little marriages that take place here every day: barley marrying water, wort marrying yeast, wash marrying heat, and the most complex marriage of all, warehouses full of wood marrying its essence to the spirit it embraces.

Budgie is beside himself as a kilt-clad bagpiper leads the wedding party up the still house steps. Mary and several of the distillery office staff have crowded into the back of the still house, and Caroline, another gift shop staffer, has stopped her tour of a dozen international visitors inside the back stairway. The group, which includes a camera-happy couple from Japan, excitedly watches the proceedings, which add a unique spark to their distillery tour.

Distilling Rob: Manly Lies and Whisky Truths

Budgie refuses to stop the stilling process for the ceremony, though in his defense, doing so is an expensive and time-consuming option. The stills are at full boil and the visitors' bodies add to the swelter. Making matters worse is the perfect weather, which marks Islay's sunniest and warmest day of the year.

If ever there were a time to blame nuptial nerves on heat, this would be it, but Hans refuses to break a sweat. It must be his German resoluteness. He stands at the decorated casks calmly and casually, as he waits for his bride, who marches somewhere behind the bagpiper. Budgie, meanwhile, limps defiantly around all the activity, mumbling as he spins cranks and adjusts the flow of liquid through the spirit safe. Despite his seeming annoyance over the intrusion, the sparkle in his eye reveals he, too, is moved by the romance of the moment.

Eva reaches the top step, wearing a basic brown dress that comes above her knees and a beige shawl with a subtle floral design. Hans, in a greenish-brown tweed jacket and vest, and brown trousers, breaks out a huge smile when he sees Eva approach. The couple is in their early forties, but at this moment they look like teenage sweethearts on the prom floor. Their small group of friends whisper excitedly to each other and one of the men, the only visitor wearing a kilt, breaks into a mini jig as the bagpiper passes by and peels off for Eva's last few solo steps to the makeshift altar.

The ceremony is conducted by a local official who strains to make her voice heard above the machinery and camera clicks. The wedding party moves closer to hear, but the guests helplessly shrug to each other as they can only catch the occasional phrase. I suppose this at least eliminates the possibility for tears. Then again, the German women are dressed like minimalistic art gallery owners and are probably not prone to easy floods from the eyes.

Mary and I stand in back taste-testing the toasting Scotch, which we know doesn't need a taste-test. She is in her forties and has never been married, and I can see how this ceremony makes her smile and perhaps even secretly long for a wedding of her own one day. I am happy that her wedding thoughts are of a hopeful future and she isn't burdened like me, with wedding thoughts of an unfulfilled past.

The couple turns around, pantomiming that the ceremony is over because no one could hear the "I Do." The officiant taps Hans on the shoulder and tells him he still needs to kiss the bride, which he does enthusiastically. Like personal paparazzi, friends and tourists rush forward to capture the moment on film. In what must be attributed solely to his cultural photographic superiority, the young Japanese guy beats everyone else, including his girlfriend, to the front of the camera crowd. Hans and Eva repeatedly reenact their sealing kiss with each additional camera request.

Mary and I pass around glasses of whisky to all the guests, including the tourists, for several rounds of toasts. Between the heat of the still house and the warmth of the whisky, everyone is anxious to leave the wedding scene and enjoy the slightly cooler temperatures outside. Even if we wanted to stay inside longer, the sweat-soaked bagpiper has had enough and the recessional music he blares bounces off the walls and machinery in an auditory urge to force people out. A look of serenity passes over Budgie as the crowd thins and the still house is once again his own kingdom.

Outside, Mary herds the single women into a mass for the traditional bouquet toss scramble. All the unmarried 'Laddie lassies stand hopefully in front, the Germans stand stoically in the back and the young Japanese woman, well, she's plain confused. Nonetheless, she stands where instructed: off to the side of the main group. Living on an island as they do, the single Bruichladdich women have very few romantic opportunities they haven't already tried, so any edge they can get, including moving a tourist to the side so they can have a better chance to catch lucky bridal flowers, is a must.

Eva wears the same post-ceremony perma-smile every bride has that says "I'm happy, overwhelmed and wow I still have so much to do today." She walks to her appointed spot and turns around with her smile facing the men and married women, and her back and windblown hair facing the unmarried hopefuls.

I've often speculated that I could make a living running a course that taught soon-to-be-married women how to elegantly, yet effectively, throw things over their heads. Eva upholds the tradition of making a throw that is wildly inaccurate and painfully ungraceful. The Bruichladdich women look panicked, the German women bored and the young Japanese woman stunned as the bouquet lands directly at her feet. She gingerly picks it up to applause and wistful sighs.

Now the look of panic crosses her boyfriend's face as people explain to him the significance of his girlfriend's successful bouquet capture. I laugh along with Duncan at the hilarity of the poor guy's reaction. Duncan moves away to again congratulate Hans, and I am momentarily left alone.

I've been to dozens of weddings in my life and served as a groomsman or best man in many of them. In all those post-vow receptions, I always made sure to slink away before the groom's version of the bouquet toss – the garter launch – happened. I wanted to be as far away from catching a marriage good luck charm as possible, probably so I wouldn't have to face the feeling that I was nowhere near finding the right woman.

There was one wedding, however, one garter toss, that I wanted to win no matter what the cost. I can still picture the garter in the air, still feel my determination and still see out of the corner of my eye the woman I wanted to make my bride. And that moment, years ago and miles away, draws my attention away from the shiny new bands of gold on Hans's and Eva's hands. I walk away from the celebration, leaving them to enjoy their dream.

THIRTY-FOUR

THE LEAP

"How badly can you 'accidentally' hurt a young child before police sirens wail and parents start beating you with piñata sticks?" I think to myself.

My friend Russell is twenty feet away, doing a campy dance to ease through his embarrassment of removing a garter from his new bride Marie's thigh in front of a hundred people. Of course, the jeers and catcalls coming from his family and friends in the open-air courtyard of this exquisite hacienda only heighten his unease. Several people bang heavy wooden sticks on the ground in rhythm to the music. The sticks are leftover from an earlier piñata pummeling that came shortly after the wedding ceremony. They are also my number one concern as Russell struggles through layers of Marie's white lacy dress.

I look to the side of the crowd and see a tall redheaded woman clapping and pointing. She's not focused on Russell; her cheering is for me. I wink at her as I'm filled with head-to-toe warmth that has nothing to do with the vino we've been drinking here all day in the Santa Barbara wine country.

Katie is luminous among the crowd, her ivory skin shimmering under the rising moon. She wears a rose-colored dress and pearl necklace that, along with her red hair and candy apple cheeks, give her the appearance of a goddess of fire and light. Her brown eyes glitter above her wide smile as the clapping increases with Russell's successful garter removal.

A few minutes earlier, Katie and I had been dancing in our own world on the dance floor. This was our fourth date. We'd "met" on an Internet dating site, which had evolved in complexity and quality from my early days of online dating. Her picture, a cross between Ashley Judd and an Irish princess, caught my attention, but it was her creative words that gripped my curiosity:

> *I will give you the "quick and dirty" on me by giving some film characters I feel most define my personality. I share: The openness/goofiness of Natalie Portman's character in "Garden State"; The passion and tendency to wax esoteric of Julie Delpy's character in "Before Sunrise"; The loyalty and sometimes grittiness of Helen Hunt's character in "As Good as it Gets"; The vulnerability of Jennifer Aniston's character in "The Good Girl"; The kookiness and wanderlust of Kate Winslet's character in "Eternal Sunshine"; The quiet allure of Scarlett Johansson's character in "Lost in Translation"...and a pinch of the disarmingly self-deprecating Diane Keaton in "Annie Hall." Kind of a strange way to describe myself, I know, but perhaps this will somehow illustrate (or act as a rough sketch) the essence of "me" for you, for now...*

I immediately raised my own self-describing saber to meet her characterization feint:

> *Like "Garden State's" Zach Braff, I can stare into the abyss and announce my existence with a primal scream; Like Ethan Hawke in "Before Sunrise" I find a conversation can be more sensual and stimu-*

lating than anything else and I understand that love-making doesn't have to entail removing one's clothes; I have Jack Nicholson's ability to make kick-ass mix CDs for any situation in "As Good As It Gets"; I have John C. Reilly's house painting talents in "The Good Girl," and I too have never gotten anyone pregnant; Like Bill Murray in "Lost in Translation," I discover things about myself when traveling in foreign countries, and I love a great whisky; I play tennis as well as Woody Allen in "Annie Hall"; and finally, my greatest quality, is I possess Elijah Woods' "Eternal Sunshine" ability to convince strange women that he's actually their longtime boyfriend. So, seeing as how you and I have been together for six months, I'm going to stop writing. But, I seem to have misplaced your phone number (and you know how bad I am at remembering numbers!), so if you could please email it to me...

Our first date was a meeting in a crowded bar, and our conversation enraptured us until the staff asked us to leave, pointing out that they wanted to go home because it was closing time. Our second date came after repeated blow-offs by her and scathing ridicule of her blow-offs by me. Our third was an evening of passionate fun in a private karaoke room that included some singing. Our fourth was this wedding, which I backhandedly asked her to and she called me a coward for not asking her outright. Four dates and we were already more intriguing than any telenovela.

All the ups and downs are behind us, tonight, though. Something clicked on the two-hour drive from LA to Santa Barbara this afternoon. It was as though we had an understanding that spending this much time together meant we could leave our fictional counterparts behind and just be ourselves. Instead of two adults concerned about appearances in front of each other, we were two kids, free to run around and play at recess. I think that's why she's challenged me to catch the garter that I've successfully eluded in past weddings: she wants to see if her new playground pal will come through for her. I want to catch it because the thought of making her happy makes me very, very happy.

Katie gives a supportive cheer for me as Russell stretches the garter for the launch. I'm faced with a huge dilemma: between Russell and me stands a five-year-old boy. I can't move left or right because tuxedo-clad groomsmen firmly hold their ground. If I'm to have any chance at this piece of fabric and elastic, I may have to plow through the innocent child in front of me. I take in the vision that is Katie and am swept with a sense of pure devotion. Death by piñata sticks be damned. I'm going to get this garter, even if it means angry parents beating the stuffing out of me.

Like a slingshot, the garter flies through the air. The white rocket arcs high above the vine-covered columns of the courtyard and is silhouetted against the starry sky. Bodies compress and a mass of males pushes forward. Cheers erupt from the inebriated crowd as the garter starts its descent. Arms shoot skyward in unison. The bottom of my vision marks where the child stands, and muscles that haven't been fully utilized since my high school track days engage. I feel the back of my thigh brush the top of his spiky dark hair as I hurdle the tyke.

I stumble forward as I land and feel the rush of disappointment fly by as the men behind me moan. A unified losers' moan. Triumphantly, I hold the garter high and turn to acknowledge the crowd surrounding the garter gladiatorial arena. The little boy still stands, stunned, but unhurt. People clap for my athletic accomplishment and groomsmen slap me on the back in congratulations. My eyes settle on Katie whose jaw is still dropped open. I walk to her.

"Remember this," I say, showing her the garter. "Remember this."

*

Later that night, after a two-hour drive home, Katie sleeps in my arms for the first time. The garter hangs like a trophy from a bedside lamp. The beauty of my present in a deep slumber. The promise of my future dangling tantalizingly close.

She is at peace and so am I. Finally. I revel in the moment. After all I've been through – the penance served to a repressed childhood memory, the awkwardness and disappointment of stumbling my way through adulthood, the personal confidence not matching the professional success – I feel, in this moment, like a whole and present man.

The drama of some of our earlier dates is far away from our bed. I only know that I already love this person who has somehow found her way into my life. I stroke her arm as I teeter between excitement and fear at this revelation. My fingers settle over a faint band of color that wraps around her wrist: a faded tattoo of a wreath of flowers. Katie started removal treatments two years ago, but gave up halfway through.

I caress the discolored skin. Katie is so beautiful, witty and smart. Why does she leave herself marred like this?

Gently, I pull her arm toward me so I can better see the design without disturbing her. I can't tell whether it looks like a scar that is trying to hide something, or if it's a bloom of flowers that is trying to rise out from the inside so it can flourish in the light of day. A thought lingers:

What if it's both?

THIRTY-FIVE

WHEN THE STUDENT IS READY

"Goddammit!" I scream at the car that's disappearing around one of the many curves of the Loch Indaal road. This is the fourteenth car in the last fifteen minutes that hasn't slowed for my thumb.

Easter is this weekend and the change it brings to Islay shocks me. I've been "thumbing" my way around when I miss buses with little problem throughout the winter, though I usually had only one car pass me every ten minutes. Today, the traffic is heavy, but instead of seeing helpful faces looking out the front windshield, I see the fearful eyes of drivers from England, Sweden, Germany and Finland who have been made paranoid by tales of homicidal hitchhikers.

The long weekend has shaken Islay from its seasonal dormancy, and we've been overrun by tourists and by the return of prodigal natives. It seems the island's population has doubled in a matter of days. I'm finally picked up by a local who nods in sympathy at my story about being ignored by frightened tourists.

"It's that time of year," he laughs.

This young man is part of a lost generation of Ileachs, mainly between the ages of eighteen and thirty, who now call the mainland home. They left to find the education, jobs and companions that are hard to come by here.

I first noticed the island invasion two nights ago when I was at the Port Charlotte Hotel bar enjoying a pint of Islay Ale, which the Lochindaal doesn't have on tap. I wasn't surprised to see tourists crowding this place and shying away from the Lochindaal down the road. The people in there are too "local."

At first, I was intrigued by the new faces and flurry of accents. The novelty quickly waned. I became angry to the point of wanting to rally the locals to form a counterattack to this incursion after I repeatedly heard the self-important demands made upon the waitresses and bartenders, and the protracted arrogance paraded by self-proclaimed whisky experts who tried to top each other's taste descriptions by bringing up examples of ridiculously old and expensive whiskies they'd tried in the past.

My island has been besieged by strangers who don't know her mystery and misery. They won't understand her instability and inner beauty. They'll rip away from Islay only the things they want to see: a welcome respite; a temporary salvation; the glimpse of a different life. They don't know her sad history, the deeply buried ruins of lives lost and left behind in times of disease and famine. A month from now, it will be another fading vacation memory for these interlopers.

Locals do a much better job of adjusting to the seasonal migration than I do; after all, this weekend marks the return of long-absent sons and daughters, brothers and sisters, friends and lovers. And, the flood of tourist dollars puts food on their plates and heat in their homes. To be fair, plenty of these tourists are repeat visitors whom many locals consider real friends.

Distilling Rob: Manly Lies and Whisky Truths

Maybe my harsh reaction stems from jealously about this fact. Visitors who are here for one week, year after year, are more eagerly appreciated than some guy from Hollywood who has invaded the island and refuses to go. This only adds to my sense isolation. I feel I am an orphan within this population boom, belonging neither to tourists nor natives.

One evening, I return to the Port Charlotte Hotel bar and I suddenly find my place.

As I walk in through the street entrance, a man in his late fifties and his wife walk into the bar across from me through the entryway that leads to the hotel rooms. His salt-and-pepper goatee, trendy glasses and single stud earring give him a hip professorial look. I stare at him for a second and realize he *is* a professor: Barry Sarchett, a professor of English at Colorado College and one of my most influential teachers. He is with his wife Lisa, also a professor. Barry and I stop and gape at each other before erupting into simultaneous conversation.

"Barry Sarchett! It's Rob Gard from CC!" I say, pointing to the Colorado College pullover I happen to be wearing.

"Rob! What in the world are you doing here? I can't believe it!" Barry exclaims.

"I'm working in a whisky distillery."

He pauses for a moment and Lisa looks at him, coming to grasp with the situation of this chance encounter on an island thousands of miles from Colorado. Finally, Barry nods.

"Of course. Where else would I possibly see Rob Gard except on a whisky island?"

Barry and I are both whisky lovers. I had the privilege of reconnecting with him in recent years while serving on the Colorado College Alumni Association Board, and we tended to wax in those encounters about our favorite drinks, Scotch for me and bourbon for him. In fact, we'd kicked around the idea of doing an alumni event where I'd lead a tasting while he discussed whisky in literature. Whisky and writers go together like Scotch and soda.

Lisa goes to the bar to buy a round of drinks, and Barry and I sit down next to the coal fire.

"I can't believe I am sitting in front of Rob Gard at a pub in Scotland. But it makes perfect sense. Why are you working at a whisky distillery?" he asks after we do a quick catch-up about mutual friends.

I explain about my dissatisfaction with the political communications strategy career, and the desire to have tangible interaction with my passion for whisky. I can't bring myself to reveal that the true purpose I'm at such a drastic life intersection is because of my internal vacancy regarding my own manhood. Though, if I were to share that with anyone, few people would be more appropriate than Barry.

He was the advisor for my senior seminar: The Adventure in Novel and Film. For the first time, I was able to analytically examine the influence of fictional projections of idealized manhood on my ordinary life. I was also one of the few people in the world who've been able to top off their college career by writing a massive thesis about Indiana Jones. Barry, Lisa and I spend the evening drinking and catching up. They are on Islay for two days following a lecture Lisa gave in Glasgow, figuring if they were this close to a whisky Mecca, they'd best make the trek.

"I don't know if you have plans tomorrow; but if not, we'd love to have you join us for a tour of the island," Barry suggests. I have the day free from distillery obligations and eagerly take him up on the offer.

I don't sleep that night, as I'm excited to try to impress Barry the next day. I arrive at his hotel twenty minutes early and nervously pace, waiting for them to come down from their breakfast. They finally arrive and we crowd in their Mini Cooper.

We start the day at Bruichladdich, where Mary and I lead them on a tour. I proceed to take them to my favorite spots on the island, explaining Islay's often tragic history and how the whisky industry threads its way through all aspects of life here. Barry and Lisa listen studiously when I describe the whisky-making process, the impact of different barley strains and barrel types, and the mysterious magic of aging.

As I see their eager eyes consume the information I provide, I realize that I am teaching the man who first opened my eyes to viewing my boyhood idols in a new light. Barry himself has a larger than life history: a Washington butcher's son who grew up to live a life of international immersion and intellectual exploration. And his eyes and ears are totally focused on me.

I'm not a tourist here and am not a native. I'm not a boy and not a man. In this moment, I am wholly me and am respected for it by a man I admire.

THIRTY-SIX

VIRTUAL DANCE

Sophie feels weightless in my arms as I lift her and spin us both in a pinwheel of camera flashes, rhythmic claps, smiles, laughs, toasts, and merrily played instruments. The petite, pretty brunette from Glasgow and I are the center of attention in a pub crowded with locals and tourists. Our impromptu dancing session is inspired by a trio of traditional Celtic musicians. The players are crammed in a corner, stuck between a table and a bench, as historic photos precariously teeter with the beat and threaten to fall off the wall and hit the musicians. The guitar, accordion and pipes make a sound much bigger than the individual pieces would indicate, and the pub is filled with jigs and reels.

Sophie is visiting the island for the weekend with Sarah, a tall, thin blonde who is originally from Islay and now lives in Glasgow. Sarah is also Aaron's ex-girlfriend. He, Jack and I stop in the pub following an all-you-can-eat steak dinner at the Port Charlotte community center. I don't eat red meat, so the decision to spend thirty dollars on steak is odd, but I've really grown attached to those two guys. They accept me for who I am. I don't have to dazzle with tales of Hollywood to impress; I don't have to flash expensive watches to intimidate; I don't have to alter my conversation to sound tough and working class. All I have to do is enjoy myself when I'm with them, steak or no steak.

The steak night chef accepts my lack of red meat consumption as a culinary challenge. Between making steaks for everyone else at the supper, he creates a smoked fishcake appetizer and a chicken pasta dish for me. I also vacuum in four servings of crepes and ice cream to top things off. I have no income, so I need to make the most of my money spent.

Later that evening – barely able to stand straight thanks to those damn crepes lodged in my stomach – I do my best to look strong and tall as I walk through the pub door and see Sophie standing with Sarah.

Aaron goes straight to the ladies, so I don't have time to think about how I'm going to approach Sophie and talk to her. Aaron makes the introduction for me. The four of us start chatting and it is quickly apparent that Aaron and Sarah's history is a complicated one, based on their body language and conversation. Sophie and I step away slightly for our own discussion about the beauty of retreating to an island in times of emotional stress: she broke up with her boyfriend two days ago.

Throughout our conversation, I notice Sophie subtly swaying to the traditional music coming from a three-piece band. With each song and with each drink, Sophie rocks more rhythmically.

"Are you a dancer?" I finally ask.

"No, I'm a doctor of biomedical research," she replies. "But I grew up learning these dances, and I love them. What about you?"

"I always have fun when I dance. Can't say the same for the people around me on the dance floor," I respond. She laughs.

Distilling Rob: Manly Lies and Whisky Truths

"Too bad there isn't a dance floor here. I could teach you a traditional dance or two."

I take a look around and indeed, there isn't a dance floor. The only spot in the bar where dancing is possible is taken up by four Dutch tourists who've placed their chairs there to get a better view of the band. If only those chairs weren't there...

"I'll make a dance floor for us!" I proclaim.

"What?" Sophie responds, noticing the obvious obstacles.

"Watch this," I declare, as I move toward the tourist-planted chairs.

Aaron, Jack and I had started drinking a couple of hours before the steak dinner and had been going strong since. With that much ale pumping through the veins, little obstacles like a few Dutchies are easily overcome.

I approach the visitors and authoritatively explain they've placed their chairs in the midst of the traditional dancing area. They are excited! Traditional dancing? Of course they'll immediately move chairs to the side!

I triumphantly return to Sophie.

"Told you it would be easy," and with that I take her hand.

For an hour she leads me through a series of Scottish dances. I add my own twists to our moves with some of the Latin dancing I've picked up through the years in LA, dipping and flipping her as much as possible in the small space. Tourists eagerly snap pictures, and the locals laugh and clap. I recognize and know enough of the people here to understand that their laughter is supportive and their claps are encouraging. Between the beautiful woman and the real connection with my fellow islanders, this is turning into a wonderful night.

Then the crepes and beer collide.

I release Sophie from a spin with a shouted, "Excuse me!" and dash off for the restroom. I don't know how much time, beer or dessert passes, but by the time I return, the crowd has thinned and the music stopped. At least Sophie is still there. I muster up enough stamina to give her a big hug and exchange email addresses. She offers an invitation to see her in Glasgow the next time I am there.

Sophie, Sarah and dozens of other returnees depart for the mainland the next day. The tale of my spontaneous foray onto the dance floor and brave attempts at traditional dancing make their way around the island. I receive more than my fair share of comments and approving, and occasionally questioning, glances.

A few days later, I email Sophie a thank you for the dance lesson, and she immediately responds with a thanks of her own, as well as a short update about how she had to go to her ex-boyfriend's earlier that day to pick up her belongings. I take that opening to respond with a sweeping discourse about relationships, expectations, disappointment and tie it all in to the spinal cord injury victims that are her biomedical research subjects.

I never hear from Sophie again.

Internet communication is a tricky thing; it's information without complete context. You don't hear tones, see expressions or have the chance to ask for details or explanations. Then again, even if you do, the answers you get may not be fully what you expect or need to hear.

THIRTY-SEVEN

THE DARKEST NIGHT OF THE YEAR

Fire crackles and sparks from the pit we've dug on the beach for our small collection of logs. Katie sits on a blanket. She pours a second glass of wine to wash down the Greek food I've picked up for this private birthday party on a chilly late September night. Stars dimly shine above a layer of fog, which has closed in from the Pacific, shutting off our ocean view but leaving the sound of rolling waves.

Tonight marks eight months since we met, as well as Katie's birthday. In that time, I've left my job as a Hollywood newspaper editor and the lifestyle perks it offers for a new career at a political consulting firm. I head up the communications team, using my background as a journalist and my lifelong experience as a truth massager to make it sound like I know what I am doing.

The job switch offers much better money and a different kind of prestige than journalism, as I work with major corporations, advocacy groups and politicians on media strategies. The career also offers a path toward tangible adulthood: saving for my own home, a retirement fund, getting a family-friendly car and taking golf vacations. With Katie, a gorgeous, smart and fashionable woman, I have the relationship part of adulthood set, too.

Or so it seems. Tonight, the air and fog aren't the only things that are chilly and obscure. Katie and I are having a hard time talking to each other, and when we do, our words are tentative and uncertain. A few days ago, we returned from a week-long trip to London – our first vacation together. The adventure was equal part romance and panic attacks, as we would take turns worrying about what this trip meant for our relationship. As much as we both wanted a future of happiness, we still couldn't completely get beyond our pasts.

Katie's traumatic childhood stories of emotional abuse, lies, affairs and divorce broke my heart and put my upbringing in a different perspective. The man I was becoming recognized the scared child in her, the one beneath the designer clothes and trendy conversation, and saw the potential of a magnificent woman. I tried to show her the difference between who she was and who she wanted to be. I challenged and supported her to fill the space between. She saw the frightened boy in me, took me by the hand and pointed me in the direction of standing tall in my own adult skin. We loved each other deeply as we fought the difficult battle to give love to the worst parts of ourselves. We hated each other for forcing us to go down paths we'd spent our lives building illusions to cover.

The gap between who we were and where we were trying to go together and individually was epic. We were like two mythical archetypes trying to cross it: yin and yang, love and hate, give and take. And like those mythological couples from Egypt, Sumer and Greece, we constantly destroyed and resurrected each other. She would run and fall. I would chase and carry. She would push away and I would pull close. I would stab and she would salve.

"C'mon," I say, reaching for her hand. "Let's go down to the water."

"I don't want to," she replies in the little girl voice and cadence that always comes out when she is overwhelmed. "I don't like the fog; it's scary."

"Don't worry; I'll hold your hand. You'll be fine." I grasp her hand. She pulls away violently and shakes her head.

"No! I don't want to go out there. It's too scary!"

"Fine! I'll walk out there alone," I spit back and march into the darkness.

"Wait! Don't leave me here, please don't leave me!" she says with the kind of terror that causes a parent to sprint to a child's room in the middle of a nightmare.

I rush back to her side.

"Why are you so frightened? It's only fog."

"I'm afraid you're going to leave me. I'm always afraid you're going to leave me."

I hold her close.

"I just followed you across the world. The only way I'll ever leave your side is if you push me down and run away so fast I can't catch you."

She silently hugs me, and I know there is an intense dialogue happening in her head, as there often is. Though she holds me close to her body, I am never allowed near the conversations in her mind.

*

That fear of abandonment, of losing something we both loved dearly, is what made us electronically obsessed with each other. We met online, we followed each other's movements, for better or worse, on social networking sites, and our email exchanges rivaled the passion, intensity and naked honesty of the letters you read about in romance novels. We would text erotic messages during the workday. Send phone photos of where we were dining when away on individual business trips. IM each other *while* talking on the phone together. Modern love.

Technology held the strings that made our relationship dance and dip as we traversed series after series of staggering break-ups and occasional unspoken side-flings, eventually to end back together in a joyful reunion. One night, a year after the beach birthday, we were lying in bed together during one of the tides that bridged the gap between break-up and togetherness. Though we trembled on that uncertain ground of a couple/not a couple, we still surfed my laptop as we lay together, checking out wedding rental prices at our favorite winery, making draft wedding guest lists and coming up with ideas for our children's names in anticipation of the proposal, marriage and life we expected to have together. That night, my heart danced to the highest level I'd known with her. I never saw the dip coming.

Days later, when looking at her Facebook profile, I saw a guy I'd never heard of before posting some mysterious comments on her page. Things that made my stomach drop, my face blanch and my heart numb. There was nothing blatant, but there was enough for me to know that the latest gray area we'd entered as we worked on some individual issues before pressing forward with marriage had taken a dramatic shift for her and now for me.

Katie assured me that it was one of those things that are misinterpreted online. She begged me to stay calm while she figured out what she was doing with her life and with us. I agreed not to cut her off. As our relationship had evolved, my heart opened itself with abandon, and I was incapable of closing it. Now, staying in her life while she figured things out put me on the verge of emotional hara-kiri.

*

December 21, the darkest night of the year. Katie and I sit distantly across from each other in a little Italian restaurant that has become "our" place. At the moment, it feels like neither of us belongs here. Though all the tables are close together, the dimly lit restaurant affords us some level of privacy for our discomfort. Between the loud music and the din of other dinner conversations, no one can hear our silence.

"Tomorrow night will be the first time," she finally admits, looking up from her untouched meal that is now cold.

I hear a dozen glasses clink across the restaurant in a toast to a newly engaged couple.

"You haven't even met this guy?" I finally whisper. "You're dragging us through hell for some guy you haven't even met?"

Katie turns her eyes down and blinks reflexively. A woman at the next table slowly eases her fingers toward her date and tenderly takes his hand as he looks over a wine list. Katie doesn't look up.

"I'm doing this for us. I need to know that our relationship is the right thing."

I drop my head. It doesn't dawn on me to ask how they actually know each other if they haven't met. All I know is the woman whose beautiful eyes used to lift me up won't even raise them to look at me.

"And this is how you're doing it? How can you do this to me? What do you expect me to do?"

She shakes her head, still staring at the table.

I have no words. I feel I'm watching something die.

The next night, I'm two thousand miles away in Wisconsin for a long Christmas break while this guy is staring into the eyes where I saw my children.

Christmas Eve, Katie emails me and reveals that she hasn't been completely honest with me about this flirtation. Some weeks earlier she'd returned to the dating site where we first met and became active again. This man's entrance into our world is not some inadvertent online social encounter caused by piqued curiosity. It is a deliberate move to replace me.

Christmas Day, I tremble my way through conversations with my relatives. The next few days I drink myself into a haze at gatherings of friends. I grow emotionally terminal with each passing minute. I return to my codeine and whisky cocktails, this time adding anti-anxiety and anti-depressant medications. Katie emails again announcing she has decided to go out with this guy on New Year's Eve. A year before, she told me on New Year's Eve that I was "the one" for her.

My family is at a loss about what to do with me or to say to me. I am a living and moving nervous breakdown. Catatonic. Unable to speak. Incapable of eating. Shuffling through movements to make it to the airport for my New Year's Eve flight back to LA. I don't feel like I am returning to my home. My world is gone.

*

I find myself at the ocean's edge, standing on a cliff below the Pacific Coast Highway as the sun rises early on New Year's Day. Warmth rolls down my back as the sun's rays descend with each passing minute. The steady ocean breeze raises salty mist to my face and sends a chill through me. Half hot, half cold. Half alive, half unliving.

The rest of the world is asleep after welcoming in the New Year. Katie is presumably in the arms of her new lover. I am

Distilling Rob: Manly Lies and Whisky Truths

mere miles from where she and I had our fateful wedding date two years earlier. I am a trillion miles from that happy and hopeful garter grab. The sea smashes against the rocks below the cliff upon which I hesitate. The waves strike with a shout and silently disappear. Strike and disappear. Strike and disappear.

All that has been my life until this moment has added up to nothing. Every persona I'd assumed through the years, all the experiences I added to my life resume, the childhood trauma remembered and overcome, and the finally discovered ability to open up and love, have failed to lead me to happiness and meaning. All that I've planned for my future is now lost. The house I imagined with Katie will never be built. The children we've named will never be born. The arms I wanted to feel around me every morning until the day I die will never hold me again.

I close my eyes and lean over the edge. Everything stops. The water ceases moving. The waves no longer crash. Wind evaporates and the sky shrinks. My body falls away from my vacant spirit.

All goes black.

Then, I breathe, deeply, strongly and fully in the present. A new breath for a naked existence.

THIRTY-EIGHT

INESCAPABLE LABELS

Eyes closed, I take in my final breath of the sweet wood and whisky that fills the warehouse. A light mixture of ice and rain disrupts the spring day behind me as I stand in the warehouse doorway, but it fits my melancholy mood. Earlier, Duncan told me that this is my last morning working with Aaron and Jack and the rest of the warehouse crew. I don't remember when, if ever, I felt so connected to my work, like it was an extension of me. The simplicity of the warehouse – my physicality, whisky, casks – elegantly intersects with this exploration of the basics of my life. This isn't a warehouse for me; it's a Zen temple.

Aaron and Jack share man-hugs with me – that half-embrace/full slap on the back that shows men's heartfelt appreciation for each other without being too dandy – before they disappear into the depths of the warehouse to continue working. I stand alone, looking at thousands of individual casks. Each wooden vessel is a diary of the forgotten people who worked to mash, distill and cask the whisky. There is so much story within each that will never be told. All people will have is the end result and will judge accordingly.

My time at the distillery is winding down and I still haven't met face-to-face with production manager Jim McEwen. However, he's given word that he wants to send me to the neglected ugly duckling sibling of the alluring whisky-making process. I'm forced to move on to the final stage of Bruichladdich's production. I'm off to work in the bottling hall.

*

Thumping machines, relentlessly clanking bottles and the grating slide of wooden pallets along cement floors assault my ears. Florescent lights droop a lifeless pallor over the mechanized march that surrounds me, sharply contrasting with the mysterious darkness of the warehouse and the celestial brightness of the still house. With automatic efficiency, workers push the buttons and watch the control panels that unceremoniously cage the water of life into perfectly conformed bottles.

John, who manages the bottling hall, is giving me an overview of operations. He talks about custom-designed bottling machines, labeling regulations for different countries and seasonal fluctuations in bottling output. He is friendly and knowledgeable, but I cringe at the thought of my whisky – the barley I've nurtured, squeezed the finest essence out of its core and nursed as it aged in casks – being referred to as "product." Cases of whisky roll by us and empty pallets quickly fill as more and more bottles come off the creaking assembly line and are placed in their rigid shipping boxes.

The bottling hall employs more than a dozen people, and I recognize many of them, not from seeing them around the distillery, but from coming across them at local pubs and shops. I know that this guy's wife works at the co-op, that woman's husband is a fisherman, and the young lad in the corner has a crush on a teacher at the high school. The people in here are full and real to me, the fabric of the community.

But unlike Thomas, Budgie, Aaron and Jack, these workers don't have the same tangible investment in the product they are sending to the world.

I'm greeted with looks of curiosity and indifferent interest. I'm an interloper in their cloistered world. The employees also aren't interacting much with each other, and I immediately pick up on subtle undertones of territorialism between the bottlers and the labelers. The dull lights that cast a naked glow over the endless flow of bottles and boxes diminish me into a pale observer of this ordered hierarchy.

I struggle intensely to connect with what John tells me, but my focus isn't here. I wish I could blame it on the production noise or the blare of disco coming from the oldies station on a nearby radio, but my problem isn't an external one. I don't know what it is. I hate being here.

We slip through a plastic curtain barrier that separates the general assembly line from the specialty labeling section, where they add regulatory labels for each country Bruichladdich is shipped to. I'm going to be working back here for the afternoon, placing labels on bottles, physically close to the whisky but far removed from its spirit. The plastic curtain closes behind us and slowly seals us into the claustrophobic labeling area, but not before I take a last look at the industrial grind behind me.

I see the large, opaque, plastic retaining tank that holds whisky gathered from a dozen casks before it's bottled. It seems like a casket compared to the living, breathing interaction these whiskies had with their casks for nearly twenty years.

Suddenly, I understand why I'm so tortured by this final stage of the whisky process.

This whisky is now immutable. All that it is and all it ever will be is now set. Nothing else will influence it. Unlike wine, it won't mature in the bottle. Once that cork is plunged into place and sealed with a foil cap, the whisky's chance to grow is over. It is literally labeled for society to consume as it will. Expectations will come from what people see on that label, and while it will meet, exceed or fail those expectations, it will never be able to adjust or alter what it is. Those who consume it can add Coca-Cola or soda water to the whisky, but that will only kill its character, not enhance it. What's done is done.

I hate this bottling hall because I realize this means my time at the distillery is also done. All this time here, trying to connect with an ancient art and the men who are its sorcerers and soldiers is coming to a close. I haven't had an existence-changing epiphany. Isn't that what's supposed to happen when you uproot your life and take a dramatic quest for understanding? This whisky is ready for that next stage in its existence. I'm not. Where is my "Aha!" moment, dammit? Where is the radiance that should be emanating from my new sense of purpose? Aren't there supposed to be a string section playing and applause deafening me when I leave this island as a brand-new man?

I tremble with visions of me returning to an office, blindly staring at a computer, spewing reports and presentations to soulless suits, chained to a smartphone twenty-four hours a day, unable to escape. Unable to live. I can't go back to that life. I can't go back to that life.

I angrily slap labels on bottles as I silently stand next to two other workers who do the same, but without my annoyed intensity. Finally one of them speaks up.

"You know, those labels you're puttin' on there...they're all upside down."

Distilling Rob: Manly Lies and Whisky Truths

I look and laugh. The labels are indeed upside down. Everything is upside down.

THIRTY-NINE

AND THEY LIVED HAPPILY EVER AFTER

I miss Katie's laugh. Not the public laugh that exuded class and charm, nor the party laugh that announced she was ready to keep the festivities going until dawn. The laugh that caresses my auditory memory is the one I heard only when we were alone. The quiet moment laugh. The laugh meant for me and for her, and no one else. It said, "I love you and I feel safe around you," when she couldn't and didn't.

Today, I wonder if I will once again be touched by it.

It's been six months since Katie started her new year and a new life with another man. My life was also born anew. I finally, truly, understood that you can experience, achieve or exaggerate everything imaginable and unimaginable, but if you rely on those things to define you and, more misguidedly, expect them to oblige others to love you without reservation, you may very well end up standing on a seaside cliff, one step from a permanent stop.

Since that day teetering above the Pacific, I'd lost thirty unnecessary pounds, started a new high-profile job at the Los Angeles Unified School District, went on a redemptive pilgrimage to the place in Ireland where I planned on asking

Katie to marry me, and reconnected with friends I'd neglected during my spiral into the emotional whirlpool that was the last few months of our relationship.

One friend I tried desperately to reconnect with was my old party pal, Chad. We'd remained friends during my relationship with Katie, but now that I was single again I found I had changed permanently from who I was before her. That life was insecurity masked by half-truths and bold imagination. Katie had purged me of the inauthenticity that pillared my previous LA years.

Chad, meanwhile, had delved so deep into the games and untruths that had marked our years together that we no longer had a common plane on which to stand. His personal adrenaline rush came from seeing how much he could manipulate truth around others. My life was centered on how much truth I could discover within myself. Our friendship, so marked by chasing brunettes with bangs and banging blondes without shame, ends with a fizzling whimper.

Katie, in contrast, is someone I cannot fully let go, no matter how hard I try. Despite my personal changes and the direction our lives have veered away from each other, the connection Katie and I share seems to be contrived by chemists who refuse to break our bond. I hate her for what she did to us. I love her for laying the foundation within me that gives me the softness to forgive her. That's why, today, after all the heartache and despair, I find Katie in my arms once more – the culmination of weeks of dramatic and emotional emails, texts and phone calls in which we've both expressed doubts about living our lives apart from each other.

Material evidence of our relationship serves witness as we tentatively touch on the couch. A framed nineteenth century book folio of Stonehenge that I bought on our trip to London faces us from across the room, its ancient image fading. A bottle of wine from our last trip is decanted on the table nearest us, emitting rich aromas of a sweeter time. Through the doorway to my bedroom, a painting I bought and was never allowed to give Katie last Christmas is a frozen marker of a direction not taken; the icy blue colors of a woman who looks remarkably similar to Katie eyeing us like a cold goddess of judgment

Katie's hair is the same passionate red, her skin still softly ivory, and her clothes are enticingly trendy. We engage in small talk and occasionally probe into serious subjects before hastily backing away. Once in a while, the laugh I've hoped for passes her delicate lips. It sounds thin and doesn't resonate in the moment the way it does in my memory. The longer I hold her, the more she seems like a doppelganger of the woman I knew and loved. Physically, she is the same; yet, she looks slighter, less vibrant.

"I don't know what to do," she sighs, embracing my hands with hers as she's done hundreds of times before. The more she caresses, the more foreign her fingers feel. "No one has ever touched my heart and my mind the way you have. I never felt so physically connected with someone the way I do with you."

"Your boyfriend?" I push through a tight jaw.

She stops caressing my hand and sits taller.

"Are you seeing anyone?"

"I've gone out with a couple of girls," I respond without elaborating.

"I just feel you're pulling away from me."

I'm dumbfounded into no response. She's the one that went from talking about our babies to cheating on the love we'd built. A year ago, I would have snapped back, and we would have spiraled into a mutually destructive argument. But, we're not here to devolve into old patterns. I don't want that. Today, I'm here to show her I've grown into the person I knew I could be.

"I may take a long break from dating. I'm thinking about moving to an island and writing for a while."

She laughs at me dismissively, and I'm drawn back to one of the reasons we had such a rollercoaster relationship. I hate when she dismisses me.

"You want to be 'that guy' who drops everything for some exotic heartbroken adventure," she assumes. "You just want the attention."

She's charging for an argument that will prove to her our incompatibility. I don't take the bait. I can't. Whatever part of me that had to pointlessly fight to prove I was strong no longer exists, exorcised with so many other demons these past few months.

"Give me a reason to stay," I speak softly, stopping her smirk. She eases back to the reality of "us." I smile at her. "Despite everything, I still love you." The words are true.

"Why does it have to be this way?" she asks. "We've gone through so much, and these last few months apart have made us more into the people we always wanted to be. If I would have met you now..."

"You didn't."

She looks at me with the sad understanding that's frequently crossed both of our faces from the beginning of our relationship: our love and chemistry are incredible. The problem is with our timing and everything else.

"What do you want?" she finally asks the question that's taken us four hours to get to. "I'm with him, and I don't know where that's going. But, what do you want?"

Distilling Rob: Manly Lies and Whisky Truths

Since we first rekindled our communication a month ago, I've only had one vision in my mind: this is going to have a happy ending. How many Hollywood movies have these kinds of ups and downs, these kinds of separations, only to resolve themselves with kisses and wedding bells? That is my goal today.

Beneath the couch upon which we sit is a small black box. Katie and I had talked about marriage in the past, but I never got down on a knee and forced her to make a choice. Today, I want to spill out everything in earnest and then present the ring for the final touch. Or so I think.

As the afternoon progresses, I struggle more and more about going through with this dramatic finale. From the moment our eyes connected earlier, the love was there, but a voice keeps popping into my head that says, "Does she deserve me? Do I want her to?"

I hold off the big ring presentation. It seems too fictional, too dramatic, for what I'm feeling. I decide to go a different route. A proposal, a plea, to spend a life together comes from the heart, not a little box.

"I want you to come home," I whisper the words I've been reciting all week. However, when they come out, they feel like rehearsed lines escaping the lips of a jilted-lover character from a thousand Hollywood creations rather than the heartfelt soul-pouring I intended. I take her hand into mine, but immediately want to let go. I don't feel like I'm in my own skin, but rather in some skin that is being shed to disappear into dust.

"I want you to end this thing you have with him and come home. I don't ever want you to leave." I pause the rehearsed beat. "I want to be thankful when I fall asleep next to you each night and even more thankful when I wake up next to you each morning. And I want to feel that way for the rest of our lives." Our lives. I stutter over those last two words.

She stares into my eyes, and I see the formation of tears. Katie, my Katie, is fully connected with me in this moment. I am completely filled with love as I recognize our long journey in her tears. Yet, the sentiments I just expressed are not living words. They are echoes of feelings.

"I don't know what I want," she finally sighs through tears.

But she did know. We both knew. We weren't here to resurrect our future. We were here to bury our past.

My heart lifts. She continues to talk, but her words fall away from my ears. Instead, I'm overcome with the realization that as much as I will always hold a love for Katie, there is only one certainty in my life: I am free to live as I want, not as other people and experiences dictate.

FORTY

DISTANT DREAMER

The distillery is quiet today. My shuffling steps make a circular echo around the inactive buildings surrounding the courtyard. Aside from the occasional pump kicking in, generator buzzing or coolant water gurgling, the scuff of my work boots against pavement is the only audible indication of life here.

The narrow opening of Bruichladdich's front gates reveals the shifting waves of Loch Indaal. This evening, the small whitecaps are tinged with purple, a reflection from the sky's farewell to the setting sun. The purple evolves into a reddish hue when it touches the Paps of Jura and the hills behind Bowmore, across the bay.

The waves slap the rocks along the shore, adding a subtle emphasis to the not-quite-silent silence. I turn away from the main courtyard and its whitewashed buildings, and climb the uneven path to the darkly stark warehouses. The perfumed sweetness of slowly evaporating whisky seduces its way through my nose as I approach the warehouses. Turning around, enveloped by the lovely scent, I overlook the peaceful distillery and the sea loch neighbor. A half-moon peeks above the hills as the sky shifts to a darker shade of purple.

This is my last night at the distillery. Tomorrow, I finally have my desperately sought session with Mr. Whisky himself, Jim McEwan, and then I'm back to the cottage for a few weeks before heading home to the U.S. I arrived on Islay with a passion for whisky and an academic knowledge of the process, and I'll leave having connected that passion with the actual art of whisky making. Yet, at the moment, I don't know what I've gained, if anything at all, beyond that.

I sit and stare into the encroaching evening.

*

Last night, I was at the Lochindaal pub for the final time as a distillery worker. I gave Matty carte blanche with making dinner for me under the strict, strict, strict guidelines that it had to be seafood. I still didn't trust him with my non-red-meat diet after the haggis incident the night we first met.

"Don't worry, my friend, I'll take good care of you. I'll take good care of you," he says in a way that eases my concern. My confidence is also buoyed after I check with the other bartenders to confirm that Matty is sober enough tonight to remember my specific seafood request.

Several dozen langoustines, a smoked mackerel, broiled salmon and lobster later, I am indeed taken care of by Matty's wizardry. I move to the bar for an after-dinner whisky and find myself sitting next to a young woman, maybe eighteen at best, with deeply sunken eyes that are on the far side of the day away from sleep.

Her scraggly hair hasn't been washed in days, and the skin on her face is stretched too tight on her weak cheekbones and weaker chin. Her teeth, preternaturally dark and jagged, sneak out from her thin lips as she sips vodka through a straw. Despite these individual physical deficiencies, the whole of her face is strangely attractive in a "Corpse Bride" way.

Distilling Rob: Manly Lies and Whisky Truths

I can't help but stare at her, which she doesn't seem to notice. I can't tell if she is drunk or has other substances flowing through her body, but her subtle smile is not connected with this place and time. A song on the jukebox ends and I watch her float to the wall-mounted machine and drop a coin in the slot. Without looking at the song selections, she types in a song number, and if my eyes are right, types the same number in two more times.

As she returns to slump against the bar, Matty comes from around the corner with a small sandwich plate.

"You're gonna eat this, girl," he demands, pulling her drink away from her. "You can no just sit here and drink without having something in you. I will no let you do that to yourself."

"I'm not hungry," she barely breathes.

"You have no eaten in two days, now eat!" he shoves the plate in front of her and walks away.

Until now I thought I was invisible, but the girl turns to me and slides the plate my way.

"You want a sandwich?" she says, more as an attempt to get it away from her than as an offering to me.

I shake my head and notice the song she picked ending. The same song starts again.

"What is this?" I ask, nodding to the jukebox. "You obviously like it."

"It's my song," she says as her eyes start to drift. "It's Duffy. Listen to it. Listen. It's my song."

And with that, she's gone again, staring into her own head, far away from the bar.

I listen to the lyrics as the song repeats a second and then a final time.

Although you think I cope
My head is filled with hope
Of some place other than here
Although you think I smile
Inside and all the while
I'm wondering about my destiny
I'm thinking about
All the things
I'd like to do
In my life
I'm a dreamer
A distant dreamer
Dreaming far away from today

The girl stands and disappears after the last replay ends. This is the first time I've ever seen her on the island and it will be the last.

*

I watch seagulls glide to the water of Loch Indaal as the purple sunset gives way to star-dappled night sky. I can't stop thinking about that girl, wondering if she'll ever be able to follow her distant dream. My thoughts turn to my lifetime of dreams that always seemed distant. I followed most of them across great physical, mental and emotional distances. Yet, I feel as lost as that girl. And I don't even have Matty offering me a sandwich for support.

The memory of one of the fictional touchstones from my childhood pushes Duffy's lyrics from my mind. It's the doll from the Christmas mainstay *Rudolph the Red-Nosed Reindeer*, looking sorrowfully to the starry sky that blankets her isolated island of misfits. I hear her sad, hopeless voice. Like her, I'm not sure if I have any dreams left to dream.

FORTY-ONE

THE TEACHER AND THE TEST

They were *gods* to me. You understand? *Gods!* Sweat dripping off their faces; fire and hammers, pure strength and power. These weren't just men. They were gods," Jim McEwan preaches with the flair of a soul-thumping evangelist.

Finally, long after he first suggested working at the distillery, I have my time with Jim. I feel as exhausted as Dorothy after her quest to find the wizard. Jim is shorter than me and compactly built. His dark gray hair waves above his slightly ruddy face as he animatedly describes growing up among Islay's whisky makers. The Bruichladdich logo on his jacket bounces up and down as his arms charge this way and that to give impact to his stories.

Jim talks about his boyhood spent roaming around Islay's distilleries where he watched his relatives and neighbors cooper casks, mash barley and work all facets of whisky. The awed youngster was sweeping distillery floors before his age hit double digits on his way to becoming a whisky legend.

Jim and I are in a smallish room near his office that looks like it's part whisky library and part lab. Glass cabinets house hundreds of small bottles filled with varying amounts of samples from casks scattered far and wide in Bruichladdich's warehouses. The cabinets are reminiscent of my high school chemistry lab where Mr. Denninger spent more time sighing heavily at the experimental mischief my friends and I would unleash than instilling knowledge into our narrow brains. This Bruichladdich lab is much more enjoyable; though, the test I'm about to take is harder than the toughest one Mr. D could muster.

Before us stand seventy-five small vials of liquid odor. Jim is administering a nosing test for me. He wants to find out if my nose can negotiate the sometimes stark, but often slight, differences in aromas found in whisky. For Jim, and for me, to an amateur extent, whisky is far more than the sum of its parts. Understanding and appreciating whisky takes on an artistic, almost ecclesiastical, tone when you have enough training and experience in picking out the individual aromas and flavors.

"What is it?" he challenges, sticking a vial under my nose.

"Smoke," I answer easily enough.

"If you didn't get that one I would have put you on a boat and made you row to Ireland," he says in a non-joking manner. We move on to the fruits.

"So, you knew from early on you wanted to work in whisky?" I continue with our conversation.

"There was nothing else for me and there is still nothing else for me," he says firmly. "It's the greatest job in the world. I get to take this delicate grain of barley, grown in a field on this island, with all its history and passion, I heat it with the best water God can give you, distill the liquid with precision that's hundreds of years old, age it in incredible casks from around the world, and bottle it right here with the sweat and commitment of Islay's own people. How could I not want that?"

"Even as a kid, though, Jim? Sweat and bottling?" I raise an eyebrow.

"I just wanted to be a cooper, like those gods I watched, shaping wood into casks and finishing the day with a dram." He looks to his own past before returning his eyes to mine. "If I could only do one thing, I'd be a cooper."

Another vial. Bananas. Jim nods his approval.

"Then, when you started at a distillery as a cooper, did you feel like you reached manhood? Did you feel like you were a god?"

He sticks another vial under my nose.

"I was just making casks, watching, listening, learning everything I could about whisky and working at a distillery."

"Grapefruit," I say as he pulls the vial away. He shakes his head. It was sour apples.

"I wasn't trying to be a god. I was trying to honor the tradition that goes back more than a thousand years. I still do that."

I have no idea what the next vial is. He holds it tauntingly close to my nose as I shake my head cluelessly.

"Quince," he finally says.

"I've never had quince. It's not fair to judge my nose on an aroma I've never experienced."

"Well, you sure as hell know what quince is now!" Jim emphatically puts the vial down.

"But, you're knocking points off my test for something I have no knowledge of!"

"Ah, c'mon, man. This isn't a test about what you know; it's a test about what you can understand and appreciate. It's a test to make you want to learn more. You can't go through life only relying on what's come before; you need to get out there and find out what's coming next. Quince. Quince is next for you."

"You've been in the industry for fifty years, and you're saying you still have things you don't know?"

"Whisky is like life. If you think you know it all, you'd better start over from the beginning, because you don't know shite."

He steps away from the vials and looks me in the eye like a father to a son.

"Listen, Rob, I'll forget more about whisky than you'll ever know. I can do more with whisky than most anyone else. There is hardly a whisky I can't save by putting it in different types of casks or vatting it with something superior. But there are some whiskies that are beyond hope. Someone didn't care enough in picking the right barley or running the right mash cycle. They distilled it too long or put it in crap casks. They didn't think about how their actions on that day would affect the whisky years down the road.

"No one knows everything about anything in life. You have to keep working to learn more, otherwise you stop caring. And when that happens, there's no hope, for the whisky or for you."

He steps away.

"I'll give you an hour to sample the rest of these. Write down your answers, and I'll grade you this afternoon," he says, closing the door to the tiny room.

I'm alone. The vials sit in front of me. Challenging me. Some contain aromas I've known and loved my entire life. Some contain smells I know I'll hate. Others will undoubtedly unleash scents that will leave me befuddled and frustrated. I reach for the nearest one, terrified that I'll be unmasked as an imposter in the skin of the whisky connoisseur I proclaim to inhabit. I shake as I remove the first stopper. I breathe in and let the aroma float into my nostrils.

Distilling Rob: Manly Lies and Whisky Truths

An hour later Jim reappears to grade my test. Out of the seventy-five vials, I am certain that I've identified five correctly. The rest of my answers will reveal me as being nothing more than some kid from Wisconsin who should have stuck with cheap beer rather than act like I'm an expert on the manliest of drinks.

Jim finishes the grading.

"You're in the top ten percent of noses. Impressive," he says.

I probably look like I don't believe him or don't believe myself, but whatever my reaction is, it causes Jim to laugh.

"Believe it, man," he says. "You've learned these scents your entire life and you'll keep learning more. What you need to learn most is to trust yourself. The answers are there, and they always will be."

He pats me on the back.

He's right. And I finally feel it in my heart. I actually know what I'm doing.

FORTY-TWO

MATURATION PROCESS

I am exhausted. My school district job is two thousand miles behind me, and I only have a few days to prepare for a move to an island off the coast of Scotland. Christmas Eve is in two days and I've yet to purchase my gifts. Despite all the tasks before me, all the fatigue behind me keeps me pinned to the bed in my parent's spare bedroom, staring at the ceiling.

This is not the same house I grew up in and these aren't the same parents I knew as a child. I'm not sure who has grown more in the past twenty odd years, me or them. Dad found pride and respect in a long and decorated military reserve career and as a leader in his church. Mom, who was pulled out of college by the plea of marriage, went back to get her degree and has held a number of community leadership positions. Both my brothers had lives that were far less troubled than mine because "their" parents got better with time. Mom and Dad became the parents I wished for as a child.

However, the exhaustion of my recent travels doesn't allow me to think about these changes. The present reality is blurred as I drift in and out of half-sleep: I'm sitting in a meeting with the head of the school district, my throat choking the words that my gripping heart sputters to say... I kiss Katie on the cheek, never to see her again...the detritus of a decade in LA is tossed into boxes as I remove the memories of girls, movie stars, embarrassing days and drunken nights from the West LA apartment I'm leaving... California quiche for lunch...Mom's roast chicken for dinner... I'm everywhere and nowhere at the same time.

Somehow, between standing at that window in my downtown LA office a few months ago and lying on this bed today, I've managed to leave behind financial security, dear friends, treasured belongings and a life that I spent a lifetime building. At the moment, this bold decision has me in the same hometown that greeted my birth and catapulted me to such tremendous adventures and anxieties. I'm rather...lost.

Footsteps shuffle to my door, knuckles knock and Dad calls my name. I don't answer, either because I lack the energy or because I lack the interest. He knocks again. My thoughts don't leave the ceiling. The door opens.

My eyes drift lazily toward Dad. He looks old, tired. Not so much physically, though he is in his early sixties and has full-on white hair. His age comes from within. The military forced him to retire from the reserves two years ago. Despite all his beautiful growth since I'd left home as a teen, his interaction with life seems to, in some ways, have retired with his age-required dismissal. He found joy and purpose in serving his country, and then his country told him to go home and stay there. As he did when I was a child, he once again loses himself and his thoughts in front of the TV. In many ways, I feel I have less in common with him than ever. He no longer scares me as he did thirty years ago, and to my shame, that lack of fear now has me treating him with the indifference he so often treated me with as a child. I don't even bother to turn my head to him when he speaks.

"Your Uncle Dan is dead."

Any malaise that's kept me down lifts as I shoot up from the bed.

"What?" I shake my head as if to make sure this isn't one of the half-illusions that have been flitting through my mind.

"Your Uncle Stewart just called and said he found Dan dead in the bedroom. Your mom is on her way to your grandma's. The police and coroner are on their way to Dan and Stewart's house."

Dad turns away and shuts the door.

Uncle Dan. The guy who allowed his friend to physically and emotionally crush me as a child. The schizophrenic former drug addict who lived with my Uncle Stewart in a house purchased by my grandma in an attempt to ensure that her two struggling sons might find a peaceful life together. He is dead.

I've no idea what to think. So much of my life was infected by the experience I had in my uncle's room as a child. After I recalled the incident a few years ago, I could only look at my already socially fringe uncle with sadness and pain. Every time we spoke at family functions, my sub-verbal conversation with myself couldn't help but question how my life would have been different if he would have stepped in sooner to save me from his masochistic, molesting friend.

Now my link to that life-altering incident is gone. Forever. No longer existing. I suddenly feel as though the entire experience as a five-year-old is now relegated to that place in the mind where reality and imagination hazily stagger between darkness and dawn.

I stand up, quickly put on my boots and grab my winter coat. It's ten below zero today and my immune system hasn't reacted well to the radical change from the warmth of California. Yet, I hurry to go out into this weather. I need to be there for my family. Mom has lost the baby brother she tirelessly and compassionately helped throughout his life. Thanks to her efforts, his last years reached some level of normalcy as he held on to a steady maintenance job and developed a solid core of bingo hall friends. She will be devastated. I want to do something, anything, everything to help her and my grandma. My family.

I rush out to make sure Dad hasn't gone anywhere without me. Shockingly, that thought shouldn't concern me.

He sits in his lounge chair, feet up, remote in his hand, mindlessly watching some golf tournament. Televised golf is almost all he can talk with me about anymore. Maybe it's because that's all his father was able to talk about with him. It's the best way he knows how to communicate with me. But his wife's brother is dead. And he's watching golf.

I stand in the doorway to the family room with a mix of confusion and growing anger.

"Are you going to meet up with Mom at Grandma's or at Dan's house?"

He doesn't move his eyes from the putt for birdie.

"She'll be fine. I just told her to drive carefully on the icy roads. She gets emotional at times like this."

I'm stunned and sickened at his deliberate indifference. He's never bonded well with her family, but damn, this is colder than the arctic temperatures outside!

"So, you're not going anywhere?" I ask with prodding condescension.

He shakes his head, eyes still hypnotized by the TV.

If I were a parent, I'd haul him off that chair, beat his ass hard and tell him to go to his room and stay there until he figured out what he did wrong. I want to scream at him. I want to throw things. In short, I want to treat him exactly how he treated me when I was a child.

Then a thought strikes me before I can strike out at him. I remember the times he yelled at me and told me I wasn't good enough for this or that, the physical punishments and the emotional distance he put before me. And I know how helpless I felt, like I couldn't do any more or be any better to be loved. I was giving the best I had, and being made to feel like it wasn't good enough devastated me.

His own wife needs him, even if she doesn't express it. This is his time to stand up and lead the family. He did it fifteen years before when my cousin died. But maybe he isn't capable of being that strong in this moment. I don't know the reason he chooses the TV over the family. Maybe he has no choice. Perhaps his emotional state is one of shock and he can't act. Maybe he's so disengaged from his life of forced retirement, of being told by his country that he isn't needed, that he can't connect with the living or the dead. I ease back from my violent impulse to yell at him. Instead, I look at him with compassion. I look at him with love.

"Well, I'm going to see how I can help."

He nods.

I turn around without another word and walk into the bitter cold Wisconsin afternoon of my hometown. Beloit is no longer the city I remember. The working-class town revitalized itself in the years since I left. The once dilapidated riverfront is now lined with parks and performance spaces. Downtown thrives with boutique shops and art galleries. They even have an international film festival. The very same movie world that drew me away from here now comes to Beloit. Everything is a role reversal. I left Beloit to find a version of myself I didn't think I'd discover here. Beloit found a version of itself that didn't exist with me around.

This is the world I walk into as I hear the crunchy click of the front door shut icily behind me. I don't dwell on how Beloit has changed. I think about how I've changed. I am leaving the house not as an angry child, but as the representative of the person who raised me with his hope that I'd be a better man than he.

FORTY-THREE

THERE'S NO OTHER ENDING

My head hurts. That's all I can think as the sun beats down upon the living room floor. I crack open an eye and spy Aaron on the couch. I hope his head hurts more. I don't bother to look for Jack. I know he's in his bedroom, and I know his heads hurts most of all.

I stiffly stand in Jack's living room, surrounded by the nicer furniture Ikea makes, and loads of Glasgow Ranger soccer paraphernalia. I don't know what time it is. Such things are hard to tell in May on Islay, as the sun rises around 4:00 a.m. – five hours earlier than when I arrived a few months ago.

More than a month has passed since I left Bruichladdich and in less than a week, I'll leave Islay. Last night, Aaron, Jack and I went out for a final drinking excursion. Actually, Jack had started drinking yesterday morning while watching the Rangers game, which explained his early departure from the pub last evening. At least I think it was early. Time slowed down as the imbibing of drinks sped up.

Time has fluctuated quite a bit these past few weeks. My days spent writing in the cottage are balanced by long, reflective walks under an ever-lengthening sun around the fields and hills I so dearly love. I've helped Dylan and his family with lambing season, feeding and nurturing lambs that were abandoned or orphaned. And, Bruichladdich is never far from my thoughts, or my lips, as I work my way through a selection of whiskies the crew gave me to enjoy when I returned to the cottage.

For the first time in my life, really, I am totally alone with me. The real me. I sometimes go days without seeing or speaking with another person. My thoughts and my experiences are my only company, and in this solitude I'm able to be with them in a way that's coldly naked and warmly comforting at the same time. I'm not indentured to a past I couldn't control, a present that is a lie or a future I don't want. I simply exist in a simple existence.

I'm oceans away from having a love in my life. My income is nothing more than the outcome of my dwindling savings. And, I feel totally free in a way I've never felt before.

The past week, I've bid my farewells to friends and acquaintances I've made on the island. Whether it's one last bus ride with Rudie and Liam; a final fish and chips at the Lochside Inn; some trampoline time with two young kids from a family that I've befriended in a nearby village; or a lengthy blather with Mary at Bruichladdich's gift shop, I know each goodbye is a closing chapter.

Even now, this morning with a hangover that won't let go, I am possessed by the same train of thought that's seeped into my life the past few weeks: What am I doing on this island?

I gave up everything to come here in a quest to discover the endoskeleton that seemed to be missing from my maturation: the backbone to shed my ever-present youthful insecurity and finally become an adult. More than that. To discover what it actually means to be a man. How to be a man.

Distilling Rob: Manly Lies and Whisky Truths

With every corpuscle in my body shrunk under the attack of last night's bottle of Famous Grouse, I look around the room. How many times have I woken up on a strange floor, in a strange bed or surrounded by strangers after a night out? Far too many to count; though, I much preferred opening my eyes to see the soft skin of a pretty girl whose name was fuzzy than I do to seeing Aaron's scruffy face across the way. Is this what I've gotten out of my time on the island? A hangover?

I shuffle to the window and try not to recoil from the bright sun bouncing off the North Sea. A couple of fishing boats bob on the waves. Men are out there earning the money they need to feed their families, to make their bill payments. Men that I am not.

I live on the same island as they, yet I am nothing like them at all. The illusion of my island sanctuary is erased with the awareness that my grand idea of escaping and immersing myself in a "back-to-basics" life of making whisky hasn't created an easily identifiable change in me. I'm surrounded by strangers I appropriate as friends, and I'm further from home than I've ever been. A transient on their island.

I thought I'd have answers about how to be a man. Instead, I am left with an absolute understanding:

No man is an island and no island can make a man.

FORTY-FOUR

EPILOGUE

Whisky is a complicated drink.
At first, it seems easy to classify and explain: it is alcohol. Alcohol burns your throat and boils your blood; numbs your tongue and weighs down your eyelids. It is this and it does that, pure and simple.

Somewhere between the Big Bang and Facebook updates, barley found its way out of the earth and reached for the sky. Monks malted it and whisky makers worshipped it.

They discovered that with cultivation, this seemingly bland seed could reveal a cornucopia of character. With the right water and yeast, it far exceeded anything it could be on its own.

What makes whisky good or bad is the care that goes in to creating it and the nurturing that goes in to maturing it. Whisky can't be categorized by practical terms. It is defined by perceptions. Unfortunately, those perceptions are wholly dependent upon an outsider's point of view.

Fortunately, people don't have the same confinement as whisky. We have the ability to find our own definition and our own meaning by altering our internal perceptions. Until our final breath, there is still time to repair what is damaged, to right what is wrong and to make brighter what already shines.

When I stepped away from that high-rise window in Los Angeles, stepped off the ferry to Islay, stepped through the gates at Bruichladdich, I wanted to see what it meant to walk like a man.

Now I know.

*

Islay shrinks away from me as the ferry rocks gently toward the Scottish mainland. The hill where I'd sit and reflect upon the world around me is now just a shadow. The steam from coastal distilleries is just wisps on the horizon. The earthy aroma of peat bogs and the fresh taste of spring berries are far from my senses.

At my feet sits my loaded backpack. It was scheduled to be tossed into the cargo hold of an airplane in a few days for my return flight to the U.S. Neither the backpack nor I are taking that flight. I've decided that the steps I started to take on Islay are going to keep me moving forward for a while. With no plan and no time frame, I'm going to carry this backpack with me on a trek through Europe. Maybe beyond. I want to take all the thoughts and feelings I've experienced on Islay and continue to distill them until they are a fully refined part of my life.

I picture what's presently happening at Bruichladdich: Thomas is staring blankly at steaming barley, thinking about providing for the son who doesn't understand him. Budgie is chattering away to the stills and occasionally hearing them respond. Jim is giving a poetic interview to an obscure drinks blogger. Aaron and Jack are somewhere in a warehouse, probably complaining that they're somewhere in a warehouse.

Within that warehouse are tens of thousands of gallons of whisky – sitting, being. Waiting for their time to come, to be enjoyed by connoisseurs, cursed by teetotalers or not given thought by the majority of people in the world.

Distilling Rob: Manly Lies and Whisky Truths

The whisky doesn't mind what other people think. All whisky can do is be what it is.

Being a man is the same thing: It's not saving the world, sweeping women off their feet or having every head in the room turn toward your charming and witty self. Adulthood isn't working in a factory and bringing home a meager paycheck with your dirty hands to put food on your family's table. It isn't throwing back beer after beer, throwing down corporate underling after underling or throwing yourself into God, family or country. Being a man isn't being anything.

Being a man is just being.

I'm not leaving with my head held high under a new crown of adulthood; I'm leaving with my heart rising high in the comfort that I'm no longer a boy looking to evolve into something I can't understand. I'm leaving with the understanding that being a man is embracing who you are, all your subtleties and fears, all your passions and weaknesses, all the layers you continue to add as an adult and all the foundation, good and bad, that was laid as a child. I am the whole of my parents' halves; their best and worst parts given to a child in an effort to make me more complete than they are as individuals. I am part of an ever-evolving process that "adults" pass on to the next generation so their children can improve upon it for their offspring.

Katie once told me that I wanted to run off to the other side of the world so I could try to be "that guy" who is defined by the escape. Now having done just that, I know she is wrong. I didn't leave to learn how to run. I learned how to stop.

I am not "trying" to be "that guy." I am that guy. I am that man.

I am...me.

I'll drink to that.

ABOUT THE AUTHOR

Robert L. Gard is a former Los Angeles newspaper editor and has written more than 2,500 articles ranging from political exposés to celebrity profiles. He is also an award winning television writer and director.

A respected whisky expert, Rob's columns and reviews have appeared in *Whisky Magazine, Patterson's Beverage Journal,* and *The Tasting Panel.* He leads whisky tastings and pairing dinners throughout the country.

Rob focuses on the relationship between whisky and writing, using whisky as an analogy for larger life experiences. Rob's pieces have been described as "writing beyond the liquid.

ROBERT L. GARD

FOLLOW

Website:	www.distillingrob.com
	www.whiskyguyrob.com
Twitter:	@distillingrob
	@whiskyguyrob
Facebook:	www.facebook.com/distillingrob

REFERENCES

Distant Dreamer
Words and Music by Aimee Duffy and Bernard Butler
(c) 2007, 2008 EMI MUSIC PUBLISHING LTD. and STAGE THREE SONGS LTD.
All Rights for EMI MUSIC PUBLISHING LTD. in the U.S. and Canada Controlled and
Administered by EMI BLACKWOOD MUSIC INC.
All Rights for STAGE THREE SONGS LTD.
Administered by STAGE THREE MUSIC (U.S.) INC.
All Rights Reserved International Copyright Secured Used by Permission
Reprinted with Permission of Hal Leonard Corporation

Profile descriptions reprinted with permission.

THANK YOU

The publication of this book would not be possible without the tremendous support of my amazing Kickstarter backers (in no particular order):

Ruth Handel
Kerri Feazell
Maricela Gomez
Saba Firoozi
Jennifer Abernathy Clark
Jacklyn & Jerry Kwon
Eric Burke
Duck Dodgers
Victor Saad
Laura Montague
Kelly C. Perler
Georgianne Laufenberg
Mark Hughes
Treena Colby
Jane Hale
Carin Castillo
Allou Rémy
Krissy Oppenheimer Caudle
Emmett Hossack
Ellen Knutson
Lucia Aronica
Carrie Banasky Dodson
Ben McEvoy

Matt Forbeck
Bruce Harlick
Angelo Veneziano
Kristie Kauerz
Vincent Wittbecker
Paulette Fontanez
Todd Harter
Joel Seeger
Chad Milton
Peter Padilla
Melissa McColllum
Veronica Perez
Rob Adkisson
Nico Spiegel
Casey Trudgeon
Joshua Gershon Feldman
Jacqui & Janet Genow
Ken Last
Raj Sabharwal
Marina Gersht
Bonny Giardina
Tim Tyler
Kristianna Evans

Julie Barnes DiFranco
Christina Fisher
Bill Burke
Ian Buxton
Jody Reed Fisher
Claudia Lorenz
Ariella Vaccarino
Jay Kerwin
Steve Hymon
Allison Regnault Patel
Nicole Rafalowitz
Kimberly Colombero
Todd McIntyre
Diane Fuller
Tiffany Chambers-Goldberg
Janet Robin
Tim Anderson
Sarah Holswade
Varun Rao
Christian Seiler
Bob Vaccarino
America Michael
Debbi Baughn
Susan Wang
Tami Schindler
Kate Hopkins
Doug Clement
Dave Smith
Mark Gillespie
Andrea Svoboda
Kat Shaughnessy Griffin

Tim McKearn
Stacey Mays
Michelle Maher
Austin Robinson-Coolidge
Sunil Rao
James Anderson
Johanne McInnis
Michael "Banzai" Bonds
Kerry Walters
Quinn Capen
Trevor Sawchuk
Dan Witzling
Eric Schwent
Greg Padilla
Mike & Barbara Feuerstein
Aaron Krouse
David Chamberlain
Richard Oster
Laura Bishop
Michelle Castillo Mohlman
Lee Vierling
Jim Kennedy
Lisa Davenport
Stephanie Molen
Abigail Greenspan
Peter Godefroy
Gary L. Gard
Jeni Schomber
Bo Smith
Randi Firestone
Nancy Grounds

Distilling Rob: Manly Lies and Whisky Truths

Matt Compton
Jennifer Rustigian
Doris A. Whitledge
Jessica Barnie
Franziska Suter
Jeff Gard
Colleen Russell
Linda Dzhema
Susan Yackley
Michelle Havel
Tara Goddard
Betsy Tate Anderson
Pamela Carter
Courtney Monroe
Aaron Trask

Greg Gard
Adam Hannett
Ann Bormett
Gary Young
Daniel Tester
Jean Jacquet
Sarah Lang
Trisha Gill
Arcelia Arce
Corey Bennett
Barry Sarchett
Steve Elder
Judith Alonso
Michael Phillips
Ann Leahy

Made in the USA
Charleston, SC
11 July 2014